# Nurturing the Talent to Nurture the Legacy:
## Career Development in the Family Business

Amy M. Schuman

**Family Business Leadership Series, No. 18**

Family Enterprise Publishers
P.O. Box 4356
Marietta, GA 30061-4356
800-551-0633
www.efamilybusiness.com

ISSN: 1071-5010
ISBN: 1-891652-12-5

# Family Business Leadership Series

**We believe that family businesses are special**, not only to the families that own and manage them but to our society and to the private enterprise system. Having worked and interacted with hundreds of family enterprises in the past twenty years, we offer the insights of that experience and the collected wisdom of the world's best and most successful family firms.

This volume is a part of a series offering practical guidance for family businesses seeking to manage the special challenges and opportunities confronting them.

To order additional copies, contact:
Family Enterprise Publishers
1220-B Kennestone Circle
Marietta, Georgia 30066
Tel: 1-800-551-0633
Web Site: www.efamilybusiness.com

Quantity discounts are available.

**Other volumes in the series include:**

# Acknowledgements

I am blessed to be associated with generous, insightful and openhearted colleagues and clients across the nation and indeed the globe. My thanks to you for being the wellspring from which these insights have flowed and in whose company many of these concepts were first developed.

Thanks to Sharon Nelton, Jane Aronoff and Craig Aronoff for their invaluable writing and editing support.

Thanks to Andrew Keyt, Executive Director of the Loyola University Chicago Family Business Center and all the participants of the Next Generation Leadership Institute who have taken on the challenge of leading their families and businesses. Thanks to Melissa Shanker, Drew Mendoza, John Ward and the planning committee for innovating the concept of NGLI.

Finally, thanks to my family for their patience, honesty and love.

# Contents

# *Exhibits*

# I. Introduction: Ensuring Your Company's Future

Nothing could be more important to the continuity of a family business than the preparation of next generation leaders—both family and non-family. Yet, career development is often neglected in family firms. Family business founders and CEOs frequently take an attitude of "sink or swim" toward the next generation. "That's how I did it," they may say. Most family business leaders want to nurture next generation development, but do not know where to begin.

*To improve the chance of survival and success across generations, a family business should engage in a deliberate program of planned, strategic career development.*

"Sink or swim" is unlikely to provide an expanding and increasingly complex business with the leadership required for continued success. Talented leaders may emerge on their own but the odds don't favor that result. To improve the chance of survival and success across generations, a family business should engage in a deliberate program of planned, strategic career development. This book will show you how.

**By definition, career development is a continuous process of building leadership capacity to meet the needs of the future.** Consider one of the saddest examples of a family business' failure to develop such leadership, the Steinberg family business. The Canadian retailing and real estate empire was broken up and sold in the third generation in large part because the dynamic second-generation leader, Sam Steinberg, had neglected to prepare his four daughters for business ownership or leadership. Only one daughter, Mitzi Dobrin, actually worked in the company. She was trained as a lawyer, joined the family business when she was 42, and with no retailing experience, was immediately put in charge of the money-losing Miracle Mart department store division. Although her father may have seen this as an opportunity for his daughter to prove herself and her leadership capacity, this "sink or swim"

*As businesses become more demanding and complex, leadership development becomes both more critical and harder to achieve.*

approach was doomed from the start. Mitzi failed to meet this challenge not because of a lack of capacity but because of a lack of preparation. After her father's death, she was forced out of the company. Later she forced the sale of the company to outside investors. If she and the business had more carefully invested in her career development, perhaps the story could have had a happier outcome.[1]

1

As businesses become more demanding and complex, leadership development becomes both more critical and harder to achieve. A family business may have a cherished vision and ambitious long-term strategies, but unless today's leaders recognize the need to give the next generation the necessary training and experience, dreams of family harmony and success can painfully pass away.

## Who Can Benefit

If you are the CEO or president of a family firm, this book is especially for you because, ultimately, you are responsible for seeing that a career-development program is established, maintained and taken seriously. You and other senior-generation executives may feel dissatisfied with the level of ready leadership in the business. If you do not know how to build the talent you need or if you are hesitant about the prospect of making judgments regarding people's capacity and performance, this book will be of great value.

Others in your family and company will find the information helpful as well. They include:

**—Next-generation family members employed in the business:** These young people want to know they will have the opportunity to grow and learn so that they can achieve their career objectives.

**—Family members outside of the business:** Whether or not they are owners, family members are justifiably concerned about what plans the business has to develop the next-generation of talent. Family members want assurance that their children will be given every opportunity to develop and prove their leadership abilities when it is their turn.

**—Members of the family business board of directors:** One of the most important responsibilities of a board of directors is to assure the presence of competent successors. A healthy career-development process will assure the future of the business. The directors may need to prod a CEO to launch a career-development effort. They may monitor the effectiveness of the development process. This book will help the board understand how to approach this critical activity.

**—Non-family executives:** These individuals often are dedicated to helping family members achieve their career goals. They may see a need to initiate or promote a career-development process but don't know how to broach the issue productively with the business owners. Additionally, their long-term security depends on the company's on-going effective leadership and they often seek to develop their own careers to the maximum extent.

**—Anyone with responsibility for a family business's human resources:** A business with a specific individual with responsibility for overseeing a career-development program will find this book imperative. Human resources professionals or an individual assigned to human resources functions will understand leadership development on a deeper level after reading this book.

## The Capacity To Support Strategy

Whatever your interest, this book will provide you with greater insight into how career development supports the strategic goals of your business and its continuity as a family firm. You will learn how to create and implement a fair and objective career-development process that meets the needs of your business and the individuals within it, and you will be given practical tools and ideas for doing so.

You will also gain understanding about your role in the process, whether you are an experienced executive trying to help a younger person, a younger person seeking to develop yourself, a board member seeking to fulfill your responsibility as a director, or a family shareholder interested in assuring the future of the enterprise.

This book will also help you become more comfortable with what may seem like a frightening process and enable you to talk with others in the business and in the family about difficult topics like a sibling who is a chronic performance problem or a senior-generation family member who is pushing her son into a position for which he is not qualified. How members of the next generation progress in their careers will have a significant impact on their individual lives and on the family as a whole.

This book is not about making a decision to join the family firm. It assumes that next-generation family members have been working in the business for a few years and have committed themselves to staying in it. This book will help them develop their own abilities and confidence in themselves both inside and outside the business. While a successor CEO may emerge from a career-development process, this

*When families and individual family members undertake a long-range program of strategic career development, they enhance their chances of achieving happiness and fulfillment in their work and their lives.*

book is not solely focused on the CEO role. **It is, instead, dedicated to the proposition that many good managers at all levels are needed to carry on a family business, not just a CEO.** Finally, this book is about developing family leaders. Leaders are needed not just for the business, but also for the family. Not everyone can be the CEO, but there are many other excellent opportunities for leadership and all require adequate preparation.

Career development is an appropriate activity for all businesses, no matter their size. While smaller businesses may have a less formal process, as an enterprise grows and its leadership needs become more complicated, establishing a professional, carefully planned program that ensures specific skills, talents and abilities are available to run the business successfully becomes increasingly important.

It takes great foresight to recognize the need for and commit to a career-development process for yourself or your business. When families and individual family members undertake a long-range program of strategic career development, they enhance their chances of achieving happiness and fulfillment in their work and their lives. One young family business president who has such foresight said, "We won't be able to achieve our business strategy without building the human capacity to carry it out. I won't be able to meet my commitments to my family co-owners and board of directors without making career development an essential part of my leadership strategy. My legacy to our family business is developing its future leadership."

# II. Unique Considerations for Family Enterprises

Because they involve family members, family-owned companies find it harder to face the issue of career development than other businesses. If a family wishes to preserve a business in the best possible condition for the next generation, engaging in career development is imperative.

Consider this common family business scenario:

A group of aunts and uncles, siblings and cousins have worked together for over a decade. Performance appraisals are not conducted on family members because they fear offending each other. Since they have never received clear, constructive feedback on their performance, they have not had the opportunity to correct flaws and strengthen weaknesses. "Relationships are difficult enough without making matters worse," they tell themselves. Instead of being clear and direct, they talk about each other behind closed doors. Larry may complain to his own father about what he sees as Aunt Dorothy's rigid style of management, or Dorothy may complain to a niece about her own brother's weaknesses. Their failure to be honest with each other becomes more and more entrenched and, in the final analysis, they and the business have lost a decade of opportunities to improve operations. For all those years, senior members of the business could have been helping younger family members develop more of their potential, and siblings and cousins could have been supporting one another's growth. The chances for business growth and profitability would have been enhanced. Instead, because of people's fears about facing one another honestly and constructively, the business is doomed to under perform its potential.

**What would decades of lost opportunity mean to your business?**

## What Makes Career Development So Tough?

Here are some of the reasons why career development in family businesses can be so difficult:

—Many families lack processes for family members to get performance feedback. They are intentionally or unintentionally excluded from existing appraisal systems. Non-family executives may be hesitant to give honest feedback to family members for fear of offending others in the family or a future boss. Career development requires feedback. If feedback is viewed as criticism or faultfinding, it may lead to hurt feelings that can endanger family relationships or may make already touchy relationships worse. Rather than being a constructive process, giving feedback is seen as potentially destructive. Lacking confidence in their skills at providing productive feedback or fearing that family members will be hurt by one's evaluation; some families avoid the process entirely.

—It's difficult to be objective about your loved ones. Nevertheless, objectivity is required if a business-owning family wishes to make good decisions about

5

promotions and job placement of family members (and non-family employees, too).

—Deciding who gets what positions can have lasting, significant effects on family relationships. Not only can feelings get hurt, but some people gain more power and prestige than others. Rivalries may intensify. Those who move into higher positions usually enjoy greater compensation leading to financial inequity between family members. Is it any wonder that some families prefer to ignore this issue, despite the fact that leaving development to chance and creating no solid basis for staffing decisions can also create conditions that destroy family relationships?

—Many families have no models or experience in planning careers. Like the CEOs mentioned in Chapter I, they say "sink or swim," or exhort the younger generation to "learn by doing." This approach is often a legacy passed down from one generation to the next. They don't know any other way. They reason that "what worked for my father and me will work for my sons and daughters."

—Business owners often place more value on customers, products, and financially focused activities than they do on planning or development, especially in the early stages of a business. "Process" functions, like career development, become more important in later stages and often aren't concerns of founders.

**EXHIBIT 1** ▐▬▬▬▬▬▬▬▬▬▬▬▬▬▬▬▬▬▬▬▬▬▬▬▬

## *9 Reasons Why Business Families Say They Avoid Career Development*

1. It takes us away from "real work," like making products, serving customers or calling on prospects.

2. We want to do it but we don't know how.

3. It would mean giving people we care about honest feedback about their strengths and weaknesses. We aren't used to doing that.

4. We don't really need to do it right now. We're okay with our current leadership. It can wait because we have more urgent things to take care of.

5. We don't have a clear strategic direction, so it's hard to envision the leadership competencies we want people to develop.

6. We tried it before and it didn't work. It took time and effort without adding real value.

7. No one helped me or my father or grandfather develop leadership skills and we've done very well. Why do we have to do all this for the next generation?

8. It is too complicated.

9. We already know who we want to lead the company in the future and they are doing just fine on their own.

---

## A Better Way

Family businesses tend to give family leaders three kinds of feedback: (1) complete silence, because everybody's afraid to tell others how they're doing; (2) overly negative, microscopically critical feedback, where every little action is criticized; or (3) overly favorable feedback, where every small action gets praised and inflated. None of these approaches help the business and, in the long run, they are not good for the family either.

What's needed instead is an open, fair process of career development. Such a process sets the stage for family acceptance of and support for potentially difficult, hurtful decisions. The impartiality of such a process leads to decisions of a higher quality about promotions and job placement for all employees. Ultimately, this process is essential for business success.

Suppose Aleta is put in a position of possibly having to fire her cousin, Armand. Armand is not performing well, and Aleta's Dad who is Armand's Uncle, has decided Armand needs to be relieved of his management position. Dad doesn't want to jeopardize the relationship with Armand's family and sees this as an opportunity for Aleta to prove herself as a leader. So he arranges to have Armand report to Aleta and urges her to hold him responsible for results and if necessary to fire him. What's Aleta going to do? She knows Armand's current level of performance is holding the company back, but she is conflicted: "Perhaps I should support Armand, no matter what, because family is more important than his lack of performance. If I don't support my cousin, I could ruin relationships in our family. But if I don't confront him, I could be jeopardizing the business and other employees who see me tolerating poor performance and cutting extra slack for a family member."

What if, instead, Aleta uses this opportunity to implement a proactive career-development process? "We're going to put a process in place where it's absolutely clear to you what's expected of you and you get feedback on how you are doing," she tells Armand. "We'll make coaching available to help you improve. At the end of a year, if things haven't gotten better, we'll have to take action. You may have to be reassigned to a job that is better suited for your skills." At that time, if Aunt Sophia goes to Aleta and says, "Honey, why did you demote your cousin?" Aleta can say, "Aunt, we had a fair process in place. We gave him a year to turn his performance around and we provided special training and coaching.

But it didn't work. He'll be happier in a position that better matches his interests and skills." Aunt Sophia may not be happy but she will see that her son was given an honest, caring and fair chance.

It's never quite that simple, of course. But research shows that when a clear, fair process is used, individuals will accept a decision that is not their preferred outcome if they believe that the process of getting there was fair.[2] A transparent, fair process can counter many of the fears that cause families to avoid career development. Feedback and decision-making become more impartial and objective, and less personal. Family members learn to be more candid with one another and gain skills in being honest without being hurtful. A fair process helps everyone understand the importance to the business and to the family of choosing the best person for each job. It can soften rivalries and help family and non-family employees work as a team. Best of all, it gives individuals the chance to remedy their weaknesses and reach more of their potential. Chapter V will show you how to create such a process of career development in your family business.

## Where To Begin

The starting point for setting up a career-development process is for the family to answer these questions: What values and goals does our family want to guide our leadership process? Is our goal to have senior management positions, including the top leadership role, be filled by family members? Or are these positions to be open to everyone, including qualified non-family employees?

If your family is deeply committed to having family members fill all senior positions, all the more reason to get started on a career-development initiative. You'll want and need talented family members fully prepared to take on the tough, demanding jobs required for a growing, thriving family business.

# III. Win-Win Career Development

One of the most important tasks of any business is to continually develop leadership capacity for the future. When embarking on a new strategy, business owners often forget to ask such questions as: "Do we have the right employees? Will we have the right employees in time to enact the strategy? What must we do now to be ready when the employees are needed?"

*One of the most important tasks of any business is to continually develop leadership capacity for the future.*

In short, **career development should support business goals and strategy. Just as you would develop a financial plan and the resources to sustain a new initiative, you must also have the necessary human resources and plans for their growth and development.** For example, if you expect to expand into product licensing, you'll need people with knowledge of and experience in the licensing industry. As many family businesses enter the global economy and expand their dependence on technology, the need for sophisticated, well-developed leaders becomes even more essential.

## Two Masters

One reason career development is so complicated is that it serves two masters—the individual and the enterprise—and each have very different needs:

**Individuals** need a process that helps them grow and fulfill their potential. They require a safe place in which to hear honest feedback, take risks, make mistakes, analyze failures and successes, be brutally honest, and at the same time, be vulnerable so that growth can take place.

**The enterprise** needs a process by which to develop and choose its own future leaders. It requires a way to objectively and unemotionally judge the relative merits and competencies of candidates vying for leadership positions. It needs performance criteria and it often doesn't have the luxury of experimentation or even mistake-making along the way.

**A well-planned career-development process finds a way to serve both masters, enabling individuals to learn and grow in ways that meet their desires and abilities while supplying the business with the performance and talent it needs to meet its strategic objectives.**

In essence, career development is an interdependent process in which the individual is thinking about "what I like to do, what I'm drawn to, what I want to develop and how I can best contribute to the enterprise." At the same time, the

9

business is considering such questions as, "Where are we going? What kind of talent and skills do we need to get there? What kind of performance will we need to expect from our leader?" When the business's needs and goals intersect with the individual's aspirations and performance, career-development becomes a true win-win proposition.

## EXHIBIT 2 ▮▮▮▮▮▮▮▮▮▮▮▮▮▮▮▮▮▮▮▮▮▮▮▮▮▮▮▮▮▮▮

## *Career Development Is A Family Business Win-Win*

| Individuals win: | Organizations win: |
| --- | --- |
| Opportunity for personal growth and development. | Clear definition of leadership needed to meet strategic goals. |
| Access to unique learning opportunities afforded by their family business. | Satisfied, directed leaders with low turnover. |
| Tools and support to better understand themselves and their career options. | A pool of talented individuals ready to meet leadership challenges. |
| Opportunities to make a significant contribution and have an impact. | Achievement of goals and objectives. |

## Three Stages of Family Employment

The next generation in your family probably ranges broadly in age. There likely are (or soon will be) teens, recent college graduates, and perhaps even those in their 30s who have worked elsewhere. All are seeking an ideal work environment and optimal career and compensation opportunities. How do you create a family employment and career guidance approach that addresses the needs of such a diverse next generation? How do you create conditions for maximum success for people with a variety of ages, interests, talents, and capacities?

It's helpful to think about family employment as having three stages, Experimentation, Entry, and Expansion:

### Stage I. Experimentation: Part-time jobs and internships.

For high school- and college-age family members, the business needs to provide carefully constructed, short-term learning opportunities. These assignments, projects, or tasks might last a week or so during a school break, or extend over an entire summer. These "experiments" allow the young family member to learn about business basics with minimal exposure and risk to the individual and the business.

Maximize the success of these internships by clearly establishing performance expectations at the start. What is the young person expected to accomplish? What are the learning goals of the internship? Exactly how long will it last? What hours

10

are expected? How much deviation is allowed? What will be the consequences if there's non-compliance? Which performance factors will be evaluated? When? By whom?

Have young family members report to excellent managers who will nurture their strengths, praise their achievements, and give constructive feedback on their missteps. Honest feedback on family members' performance from the very beginning is essential to their future success. Good work habits are best taught at the very beginning of a young person's career.

### Stage 2. Entry: The first "real" job in the family business.

Most family business professionals, recommend that family members complete a college degree and gain several years of work experience outside the family business before coming on board. Working in another company provides "real world" experience, and offers the young person confidence that they are not dependent on the family business for employment but can "make it" on their own.

Many family members return to the family business rather quickly for their first "real" job. Others might enjoy great success in another chosen field for a longer period and, for various reasons, decide to return and apply their skills to the family company in mid-career.

Too often, however, the next generation's full-time entry into the family business is mishandled. The young person is thrown into a job with minimal definition, unclear reporting relationships, and nonexistent performance feedback—the typical "sink or swim" situation. Unfortunately, many talented young people drown in these circumstances. Here are some dos and don'ts for this crucial stage:

> **DON'T** start her too high, too fast. No matter how brilliant you think she is, she's just starting off her career. Hiring a family member right into a title of "Vice President" or putting her immediately on the Management Committee does nothing to build her credibility with others in the company, and it leaves no room for growth.

> **DON'T** start him too low to prove that "family is no better than anyone else at this company." If he's a college graduate with a few years of working elsewhere under his belt, he's not going to last long stocking shelves.

> **DON'T** start her career with an extremely challenging, high-visibility project that no one else has been able to get to, with crucial implications for the future of the company. This could very well be a formula for public embarrassment of a fairly green family member who is still learning the ropes. (Remember the sad story of Mitzi Dobrin, the daughter who was tossed much too early into the job of turning around a company division.)

**DON'T** start him at a remote location, away from the central functions and challenges of the business. Growth and education is of utmost importance at this point in his career. He needs to be close to the center in order to absorb the corporate culture. There will be time later for him to get experience at distant plants or offices.

**Don't try to map out her entire career from the start.** In the early stages, maintain flexibility and consider one or two steps at a time.

**DO** find a job that matches the young person's skills and interests. Be sure it's a position that provides a view of important business functions.

**DO** make clear what the performance expectations are and what the young person should learn from the entry-level position.

**DO** name as supervisor a non-family manager that knows how to nurture talent and encourage the best in others and who will provide honest, constructive feedback.

**DO** begin to map out the next steps of the young person's career-development process early on.

### Stage 3. Expansion: Proactive career and personal development.

Leading public companies are often known for the excellent learning and development opportunities they offer their people. Unfortunately, many family-owned companies pay little attention to the careers of family members who seriously commit their work lives to the family business. This can lead to stagnation, discouragement, and even depression as family members celebrate their 10th, 15th, and 20th anniversaries in the business without any new challenges or opportunities in sight.

Someone needs to keep watch over family members' careers. Are they getting a mix of operational and staff experience? Are they getting exposure to the most impor-

*Experimentation, entry, and expansion—thoughtfully planned, carefully monitored, and objectively implemented—offer perhaps the best prescription for assuring capable family business leadership in future generations.*

*Take advantage of the flexibility a family business can offer and the emotional connection, or "heart," that it represents.*

tant aspects of the company? (Once past their entry jobs, family members profit from experience away from company headquarters.) If problems arise, are they getting timely, honest feedback and support to turn them around? Are they communicating well with all stakeholders— management, family and board? In family business, giving young leaders constructive feedback is a real challenge. A planned career-development process can help meet that challenge.

Experimentation, entry, and expansion—thoughtfully planned, carefully monitored, and objectively implemented—offer perhaps the best prescription for assuring capable family business leadership in future generations. You will find more discussion about Experimentation stage family members in Chapter IV, "Catch Them While They're Young." In Chapter V, you'll learn how to create a win-win career-development process, and Chapter VI will offer you additional tools for supporting the growth of young family members in the entry and expansion stages.

## Take Advantage of Family Business Flexibility

Let's add one more "do" to that list of do's and don'ts suggested earlier, and it is important:

> **DO capitalize on what it means to be a family business when it comes to career development. Take advantage of the flexibility a family business can offer and the emotional connection, or "heart," that it represents.**

If you're a member of the younger generation, this means taking time to articulate and fully understand the opportunities offered by your family's business ownership. If you fully appreciate what's available to you in your family's business and you commit yourself to preparing yourself for the responsibilities that lie ahead, a career in the family enterprise can be without parallel in terms of challenges, rewards and satisfaction.

If you are a senior family member, it can mean using the flexibility of a family business to be responsive to members of a new generation who look at work and at their careers in a different way than your own generation does. Members of today's younger generation tend to view their lives in a much more holistic way than their predecessors. While work is extremely important to them, they are often unwilling to sacrifice family life for an 80 hour work week. They expect more balance between work and personal life than their parents and grandparents did. Fortunately, there are many opportunities in family businesses to adapt to those expectations without compromising business effectiveness. Lara was recently named as president of her family's real estate management company.

Earlier in her career while her children were infants and pre-schoolers, she worked part-time in jobs that focused on research and market analysis. She did not take on responsibilities that entailed extensive time demands from customers that would interfere with her need to be flexibly available to her young children. The senior generation was wise enough not to bar her from aspiring to the top just because she chose an unorthodox path to get there. Once her children were in school, she assumed more responsibilities, longer hours and proved her competence, developing into the next generation leader.

Senior family members may also want to consider challenging the conventional wisdom that says jobs should not be created especially for family members. Many families take pride in saying, "We only hire family members when there is a bona fide job opening. The next generation has to fit into the position that's available." Certainly we do not advise creating jobs just because they're family and can't get a job elsewhere. But sometimes, a family will make a place for the next-generation family member who has an enormous talent, allowing experimentation with new opportunities for the business. Why not be creative and establish a position to take advantage of a great skill if it will benefit the business and the family, even if the approach is nontraditional?

A family business can adapt to the unique needs and talents of family members, and can extend that adaptability to non-family employees as well. To do otherwise may be to squander valuable opportunities.

Two more do's:

> **DO** create basic organizational employment structure, plans and policies and then stick to them, and

> **DO** set up more means of communication than you think you need. This may include: family newsletter; website; a broadcast newsletter and regular agenda items for family meetings.

Emphasizing communication helps a family guard against taking things for granted and supports the plans and structures you create. When you have these in place, don't cut corners. A family member may say, "We had an employment policy but we didn't follow it because..." If you don't adhere to your plans or you change the rules because of special circumstances, then you're ignoring the good, hard work that you have already done. Don't waste it.

# An Overburdened Grandson

W.K. Kellogg, the founder of the Battle Creek, MI cereal empire, dreamed of creating a dynasty. But in 1925, a conflict drove W.K. to demand that his son and heir apparent, John L. Kellogg, an engineer, resign from the family business. The parting proved amicable, however, and when John L. started a business of his own, W.K. was supportive.

W.K., however, turned his sights on his favorite grandson, 14-year-old John L. Kellogg, Jr. W.K. and the boy loved to talk about business, and the senior Kellogg enjoyed taking him to the plant and explaining the intricacies of cereal production and other aspects of the enterprise. John was not yet sixteen when his grandfather promised him that he would one day head the company.[3] W.K. consciously sought to curb himself from pushing the boy too hard during his teen years. But he seemed to lose all sense of restraint once young John graduated from the Babson Institute. Not long after, he was named a vice-president of the company. He sat in on board meetings and served on important committees and was charged with a plethora of complicated duties. Said one observer: "[W.K.] gave the young man a tremendous responsibility and tried to develop John so fast that his resources were taxed to the utmost…He knew the fate of the company hinged on his young shoulders."[4] When John began to experience ill health, W.K. recognized that he was pushing the young man too hard. He took John's vice-presidency away and assigned him to sales, which John disliked, and finally to the company's experimental laboratory. Like his father before him, young John found himself in a conflict with W.K., resigned from the family company and started his own enterprise. He was just 26. W.K. Kellogg's hopes of creating a family dynasty in the business were dashed forever. John died unexpectedly at an early age. It is possible that pressures put on him by a grandfather he loved and their subsequent falling out both played a role in the Kellogg tragedy.

# IV. Catch Them While They're Young

The owner of a real estate business takes his three children, all under 10, on a weekly walk around the buildings that the family owns. As they walk, they play a game: For every needed repair a child spots—burned out light bulbs, stained carpets, cracked tiles—he or she gets a dollar. Sometimes it's the youngest, a 4-year-old, who earns the most.

This exercise has multiple benefits: Time spent together; connection to Dad and the family business; teaching attention to detail and continuous improvement; a sense of usefulness, value and competency on the part of the children; a taste of what people do in the family business, and more.

*You must spark the children's interest in and enthusiasm for the family's business while they're young.*

It's important to give substantial attention to involving and teaching young family members during the experimentation stage, and, as this little story suggests, experimentation can begin as early as you want it to.

What, you may be wondering, does this have to do with career development? The simple fact is: you must spark the children's interest in and enthusiasm for the family's business while they're young. Otherwise you won't have any next-generation family members to develop for future leadership positions.

**Many smart business-owning families create a Next-Generation Involvement and Development Program as a precursor to career development. Such initiatives produce higher-quality candidates for the career-development process and help assure that there will be family members in the pipeline for roles in the family business.**

## Start Early and Make It Fun

It is important to begin next-generation involvement and development at an early age. A number of families make it a point to teach basic business and money management concepts to children as young as 4 or 5. The ultimate goal is to help young people understand, by the time they're teenagers, that someday they are going to own the family business and what that will mean for their lives.

But for now, before they are teens, the youngsters' exposure to the business should mostly be fun. Some families conduct tours of the business for younger family members and make it a delightful experience. A food company might have a special food tasting for the children at the end of the tour, or clothing company might make special T-shirts or caps as souvenirs of a visit to its manufacturing plant.

Like the father above, you can make a game of the learning you want to impart.

How about a scavenger hunt, with all the items to be collected or found being something related to the business? Or a game in which the children are asked to name as many of the products your business makes or sells as they can?

You can tap the children's creative juices as well. Ask them to make collages or do drawings or paintings that represent the values of the family. Use raw materials or finished products from the business. Turn a hallway or conference room at the office or the family's summer home into an art gallery by hanging the children's artwork there.

Invite Grandma and Grandpa over for a big family dinner and have them tell their grandchildren what it was like to start the business all those years ago and how things have changed since then. Children love photographs, so it's a good idea for grandparents to share family and business pictures from the early days.

Another idea is to ask a teenager to write a simple play about the founding of the business and have the younger children stage a performance.

Many times young family members can learn about the values that guide the business while doing good deeds for others. Grandchildren can gather annually to conduct a philanthropic project together along with their parents, aunts, uncles and grandparents. A clear relationship can be drawn between the success of the business and the values being experienced among the next generation.

## As They Grow Older

As mentioned in Chapter 3, the Experimentation Stage is the time to introduce young people to work experience in the family enterprise. This can be done without aggressive pushing or demands on the next generation which can have the opposite effect to what is desired. Make it age-appropriate. Middle school or junior high kids can do simple after-school or summer jobs, like filing or stocking shelves. High school students can take on more responsible summer and holiday jobs, such as staffing the cash register, clerking, or making deliveries. Internships can be designed for college students, with greater levels of challenge. Resist the temptation to put your college-student sons and daughters in manual jobs (i.e. mowing the grass or sweeping). You want to attract them to the business and you want each job to provide some learning.

By the time they're teenagers; young people can also begin to participate in family meetings. Consider asking all the children who had recent summer jobs or internships in the family business to give a brief report at the next family meeting on what the goals were, what they did, what they learned, and what their most memorable experience was. That kind of assignment will reinforce what they learned and give them an opportunity to develop communication skills. It will also help attract younger family members to consider working in the business.

## Equal Access for All Children

Often, summer and holiday jobs go disproportionately to the children of family members who work in the business. Consider this fairly common scenario: Joanne, the oldest child, joins the business and things just don't work out. As the first of the offspring to go in and try to make a place for the next generation, she draws all of Dad's fire, as they just don't see eye to eye. Joanne leaves and finds a job in another city, where she marries and starts a family. In effect, however, she has forged the path for Colin, her younger brother. By the time Colin enters the business; Dad is more patient and now has some experience working with next generation. Colin does well, so well, in fact, that he is named president.

About this time, the two siblings' children are becoming young teenagers. Colin's two oldest express an interest in working in the family business and summer jobs are found for them. But even though Joanne is a shareholder, her son, Andrew, an exceedingly bright 16-year-old, never expresses a similar interest. And why should he? The family business was never discussed much at home because neither of Andrew's parents was involved and Andrew's family does not live in the town where the business is located.

Colin's children are now in a better position than Joanne's son to present themselves as candidates for career development and eventual succession in the family firm—even though Andrew may have more potential. Some cousins had the opportunity to start working in the business as teenagers and others did not. Joanne, always resentful that she did not get to fulfill her early desire to work in the family business, now realizes that her son won't get that chance either. She develops an icy and distant attitude toward Colin and his children and the shareholder group is weakened.

**It's crucial that the children of all family owners have equal access to jobs in the family business and other Next-Generation Involvement initiatives. If they don't, family resentment and tensions can ensue. In addition, the family business may lose forever the opportunity to develop some terrific talent in the next generation.**

Early on, family meetings can provide a forum for developing a family employment policy.[5] "How can we provide equal access to opportunities in the business for all younger family members prior to the time for serious career development?" This might lead to a discussion of, among other things, how to provide opportunities to teenagers whose parents don't work in the business and live across the country. Cousin Tim may choose to go spend the summer with Uncle Paul and Aunt Sonia, who live where the business is located, so that he can have the chance to work in the family firm next summer. Suzanne might spend a semester studying near the business' southern distribution center so she can also serve as an intern in the family business.

## Two Committees at Work

Some business families have both a Next-Generation Involvement Committee and a Career Development Committee. Obviously, the next-generation activities will transition into a career-development process, so it's important that the two committees interface with each other. The Career Development Committee, whose duties may include developing a Family Employment Policy as well as providing input to the company's career-development process, can keep the Next-Generation Involvement Committee informed of strategic business directions and emerging leadership needs. In turn, the Next-Generation Involvement

Committee can generate excitement in the shareholder group for the early preparation of future shareholders and potential candidates for career development.

## How One Family Does It

Many of the shareholders of U.S. Oil Company, Inc., a family business based in Combined Locks, WI are under majority age. As a result, the family takes a special interest in its young people and has created a Next Generation Ownership Development Plan, aimed at developing effective owners who are now between the ages of 4 and 24. It also addresses some career development issues. Below is the core of the plan. You will also learn more about U.S. Oil and meet one of the family members in Chapter IX, "Family Leaders Need Development, Too."

**EXHIBIT 3** ████████████████████████████████████████

# *Overview*

The primary goal of the Owner Development Committee of the U.S. Oil Owner Council is to seek to provide opportunities for shareholders of U.S. Oil Co. to become more educated and effective owners. We believe that this effort should include our youngest shareholders, offering them ongoing opportunities to learn about the business, to interact with the shareholder group and to explore ways they can become directly involved with both the activities of the business and the shareholder group. The following plan sets forth a series of goals and the desired outcomes as well as an action plan for developing effective owners who are between the ages of 4 and 24. This plan is intended to be a work in progress— changing over time as the needs of the business and the family change.

The success of this plan hinges on the participation of all shareholders, but in particular the support and involvement of parents. The development of such a plan assumes that parents share in the desire that their children become educated and effective stewards of U.S. Oil Co. and are continually providing opportunities within the home environment to develop such skills.

# U.S. Oil Company, Inc.
# Next Generation Owner Development Plan

### Goal Statements for All Shareholders Age 4 to 13
—Shareholders will be *exposed* to the business and family values and legacy.
—Shareholders will experience *enthusiasm and excitement* around involvement with the family and the family business endeavors.

### Activities for Shareholders Age 4 to 7
—Social time with family, cousins, etc.
—Tour the company facilities with older family members.
—Expose young shareholders to simple business concepts through games, home activities and projects, and an introduction to money management.

### Activities for Shareholders Age 8 to 13
—Social time with family, cousins, etc.

—Tour the company facilities with older family members.

—Expose to increasingly complex business concepts such as the role of advertising and marketing, laws of supply and demand, while continuing to reinforce the value of money and money management.

---

### Goal Statements for All Shareholders Age 14 to 17
—Shareholders will become *directly involved* with the business and the family values and legacy.

—Shareholders will continue to experience *enthusiasm and excitement* around involvement with the family and family business endeavors.

### Activities for Shareholders Age 14 to 17
—Social time with family, cousins, etc.

—Tour the company facilities with older family members.

—Educate about and encourage involvement with summer internship program (depending on age).

—Offer opportunities for direct involvement with family philanthropy and charitable endeavors.

—Encourage involvement in mentoring or partnering programs with adult shareholders related to college choice and career interests.

—Encourage participation in peer groups during Shareholder Meeting.

---

### Goal Statements for All Shareholders Age 18 to 24
—Shareholders will participate in activities designed to *broaden their experience* with business mechanics and the business environment.

—Shareholders will continue to experience *enthusiasm and excitement* around involvement with the family and business endeavors.

### Activities for Shareholders Age 18 to 24
—Social time with family, cousins, etc.

—Tour the company facilities with older family members.

—Expand opportunities for involvement with family and non-family business beyond U.S. Oil through internship and other work experiences.

—Offer opportunities to guide career development and career choice.

—Teach skills such as resume development and interview skills.

—Offer educational opportunities related to understanding investing, reading financial statements, understanding the role of family governance structures, as well as the roles of owners, managers and directors.

Reprinted with permission of Sarah Schmidt, U.S. Oil Co., Inc., 2004.

# V. Creating a Career-Development Process

Let's assume that you and other family shareholders and managers have agreed that it would be desirable to put a career-development process in place. Perhaps there are now three or four bright and eager next-generation family members in the business. They are in their mid-to-late 20s, have college degrees and all worked elsewhere for at least three years, getting valuable experience, before joining the family firm. In addition to these young family employees, there are also several talented non-family employees in the same age group.

Before you embark on a career-development program, remember your goals:

—To prepare competent, qualified leadership to assure business success in the future.

—To create an objective, impartial, open and fair process that does three things: (1) builds trust and creates a process for family acceptance of and support for promotion decisions in the business; (2) benefits both the individual and the company; and (3) leads to optimal decisions about job placement of family and non-family employees, ultimately defining the leadership structure for the next stage in the family business.

## Four Stages

There are four major stages to creating a fair and open career-development process. Each stage has several steps. While the top leadership of the company (including the board of directors) is ultimately responsible for the process, one executive, often the manager of human resources should have ultimate responsibility. If you do not have the capacity on your current staff, you could have a human resources consultant, one that understands family business create and manage much of the work involved.

Here are the elements of the career-development process:

### Step One: Envisioning future leadership needs.

Visioning the future means determining where you want to go as a business and then deciding what people will be needed to get there. You begin by saying, "Here's our desired future state regarding our enterprise and its leadership."

1. The family has articulated guiding beliefs and values for the company. Family members also have agreed on a company vision—that is, they have described the kind of business they want to have and the results they hope to see as owners. A family employment policy expresses the family's desired direction regarding filling key positions, including the CEO post. The policy will specifically deal with whether family or non-family executives will be most appropriate for posts. The board of directors and management team recognize their responsibility for developing the next group of company leaders. Key non-family executives understand their opportunities related to top leadership positions and can plan their own careers accordingly.

2. Top management, directed by the board of directors, crafts a strategic business plan in accordance with the family's direction. This strategy and the company vision imply a picture of future leadership. Different strategies require different skills. One strategy might require experience in managing multiple locations and another may require greater financial acumen.

3. Management should envision the company's future leadership needs. Brainstorm with your board or your management team to identify specific competencies required for future success. A variety of tools are available to help with this process and are listed in the Resources Section at the end of this book.

Ultimately you will prioritize and list the top desired competencies for the future. You'll have to think about such questions as, "What is more important to our strategy, self-development or driving for results? Peer relationships or motivating others? Caring about direct reports or innovation management?" Each member of your senior management team, for example, could list top competencies of his or her ideal leader. Some people choose to emphasize the competencies they view as company weaknesses, hoping to strengthen them. Others pick what they perceive as strong qualities that they value and hope will continue to be company strengths. By comparing results, a final list of competencies can be compiled.

Lominger Limited, Inc., of MN offers a deck of cards called its "Leadership Architect® Competency Sort Cards," that identifies 67 different leadership competencies—such as "Action-oriented," "Composure," "Decision quality," "Listening" "Patience" and "Planning." Each card offers a description of its competency. On the reverse side is a description of a competency when it is weak or over-used. You can also use the cards to focus your thoughts about the leadership needs of your organization. The Lominger cards are available for around $75 (www.lominger.com). Alternatively, you can brainstorm with your managers and create your own set of cards, made up of leadership competencies that you find especially relevant to your business.

You will find such tools helpful throughout the entire career-development process. The Lominger cards, can also serve as an aid in setting development goals for individuals and giving feedback.

4. Review management's set of top leadership competencies with the board of directors. Gaining board approval will assure that management and the board are aligned on competency goals. Involving the board also ensures its support for the career-development process as it moves forward. Reviewing the chosen leadership competencies gets family members and outside directors appropriately involved. Board members typically welcome the career-development process because it helps them do their jobs better.

**Stage Two. Assess current leadership against the desired future.**

This stage entails identifying a small select group of your key managers and employees and assessing them against the desired future. This assessment will often have several dimensions, including a self-assessment component as well as assessment by others.

One proven method for assessing current leadership is through something human resources professionals call "360-degree feedback." This means getting feedback from all directions: a self-report from each individual plus input from all the people he or she interacts with in the company—bosses, peers, and subordinates.

You can conduct an assessment using instruments offered by companies specializing in leadership development, create your own assessment tool, or you can hire a consultant to conduct the assessment. The self-assessment process can be just as simple as having the CEO and others saying "Here's how I think I stack up on these five competencies, on a scale of 1 to 10." There are advantages and disadvantages to each approach so carefully weigh your options before getting started.

Remember, this is solely information gathering at this point. You are just collecting data. Keep in mind that the information you receive from this feedback represents how the individual is perceived by themselves and others. For a more objective assessment of the individual, you may include measurement of his or her performance against measurable business goals. Still this approach leads to the development of a kind of inventory or sketch of the managerial resources currently available in your company—a way to assess executive strengths and weaknesses individually and overall. This information allows you to proceed to Stage Three.

**Stage Three: Conduct a "gap analysis" and actively plan and pursue individual growth and development.**

1. Each individual now does a "gap analysis," assessing how his or her current performance compares to the state of leadership desired for the future. In other words, once you have assessed the current state of your leadership based on the information you have gathered, and compared it against the state of leadership that you desire for the future the gaps between "today" and "tomorrow" become clear. By compiling your inventory of collective managerial strengths and weaknesses and comparing it to the company's projected future needs, a gap analysis can also be prepared for the company as a whole.

2. Based on the identified gaps, each person creates an Individual Learning Plan that defines how they will fill the gap. The Individual Learning Plan also creates a tool for ensuring that the plan is enacted. Exhibit 4 is an example of a learning plan and can be found on page 27.

3. Individuals now pursue growth and development as specified in their Individual Learning Plan. They may seek assistance for their effort in the form of coaches and mentors, and meet with them regularly to monitor progress and chart next development steps. This process is covered in detail in the next chapter.

4. Individuals should share progress on their Individual Learning Plan with their supervisors to ensure they continue to grow and develop.

**Stage Four: Re-assess, celebrate improvement, and plan the next cycle of development.**

1. At a predetermined time, management needs to evaluate individual and organizational progress. Some family businesses create a "continuity task force" to meet regularly to review progress on career plans and development. This task force may be a committee of the board or it may be a management task force. Whatever the makeup, it should monitor the career development of key family and non-family executives. It should also determine if new participants should be included in the process and if new or revised leadership positions should be added, and set a target date for evaluating leaders at all organizational levels.

2. Everyone involved understands that this is an ongoing process that will shift focus as people develop and needs change, but some attention will allows be needed.

**One Way To Do It**

A family firm can implement the four-stage process in any number of ways, from simple and casual to more formal and structured. Here's one example of how the process might work in a more structured situation:

An outside consultant or coach is brought in to work with the top management team—perhaps the chief executive officer, the chief financial officer, the head of human resources, the head of operations, and the head of sales. This five-member team identifies the key competencies that they believe will be needed in ideal leaders of the future. The team serves as the company's continuity task force. Now that the desired state is defined, it is time to assess current leaders. A small group of key managers are identified for assessment.

Each member of this group asks three to five others to participate in providing 360-degree feedback on him and also completes a self-assessment. Computerized forms are provided and, once filled out, are sent electronically to an outside human relations company for analysis and compilation. In this way, those who provide feedback are assured of anonymity.

A report on each individual is sent to the consultant, who meets with all of them as a group and congratulates them on completing the initial feedback process. The consultant then schedules a private two-hour session with each to discuss the individual's feedback report. The consultant and individual explore such questions as: What is this report telling us? Do people see you (the individual) as you see yourself, or are there gaps? Do you recognize that your bosses see you very differently from the way your peers do? What can we make of the fact that your direct reports see you much differently from how you see yourself? Gaps are identified between the desired leadership skills and the actual leadership skills.

Out of the discussion, each manager creates an Individual Learning Plan that identifies three-to-five areas that he or she will focus on over the next year, building on certain strengths or improving on specific weaknesses.

Suppose Rob recognized that he needed to work on improving communications with his peers, direct reports, and boss; delegating more effectively and empowering others; and improving relations with customers. On a calendar-like grid, he'd list his goals and, in a box for each month, he'd fill in his progress or his next steps. Here, in a simple version, is what his Individual Learning Plan might look like:

**EXHIBIT 4** ████████████████████████████████████████████████

## *Sample Individual Learning Plan*

| <u>Assignments</u> | <u>June</u> | <u>July</u> | <u>August</u> |
|---|---|---|---|
| 1. Pay attention to communication with boss, peers and reports. Strive to be encouraging and proactive. | Boss & peers, 30% reactive; reports, 55% reactive. Work on complimenting others. | Good progress in becoming more proactive and less crisis oriented. | Watching balance of negative comments vs. positive. Some improvement since June. |
| 2. Move from solving problems to creating employee capacity to do so. | Worked on listening, not jumping in with my own ideas all the time. | Worked on cultivating patience needed to let others take on new tasks. | Patience still needs work. But Sue came up with a great solution to marketing problem. |
| 3. Visit 4-5 customers per week to establish greater rapport & learn about their needs. | Busy work schedule. Made only 2 calls per week, but good ones. | Still no more than 2 calls a week. Need to discuss schedule with boss. | Discussed need for more time for customer visits with boss. Still to be resolved. |
| 4. When communicating with top management use "benefits" language. | | | |

*An organization that is trying to focus on career development has to find ways to recognize and reward middle and top managers for being career developers.*

Someone else might choose to make the Individual Learning Plan even simpler, filling in four columns: "Skills I Need To Develop," "Action Plan for Doing It," "Whose Support Do I Need To Make This Happen?," and "Results."

The management team or continuity task force meets regularly to assess the progress that has been made in developing leadership for the future and to decide on next steps, such as doing another round of 360-degree feedback and inviting other potential leaders to participate.

## Separating Career Development From Evaluation

It's important to keep career development separate from performance appraisal. Career development needs to be viewed as a non-punitive process, one in which people can be vulnerable, take a honest look at themselves, and safely grow and learn without fear of job loss. People worried about being evaluated find it difficult to be completely open to corrective input.

Because the appraisal process impacts promotions and compensations, people often pay more attention to it than to career development. To put "teeth" into a career-development effort and get people's attention; it also needs to be part of the promotion and reward system—not of the person being developed, however, but of his or her boss. People tend to do what gets measured and rewarded. An organization that is trying to focus on career development has to find ways to recognize and reward middle and top managers for being career developers. Part of their performance appraisal should include assessing how well they develop the careers of those who report to them.

## Three Dilemmas

Family-owned businesses face three dilemmas when it comes to career development. How each dilemma is resolved will be different in each organization, depending on its nature and its circumstances. However, wise families give thoughtful consideration to these dilemmas and prepare for them.

### Dilemma #1: Who "owns" the information?

Who does the feedback and other assessment information belong to? What is the level of confidentiality? How will the information be used? These questions need to be decided in advance and shared with all concerned, including people going through the process, people conducting it, managers and board members. Everyone needs to know the rules and no one should be surprised.

In some cases, board members who are charged with making a difficult succession decision may be eager to acquire information on potential leaders and how their skills are developing. It should be clear to the board when and if such information will be made available. They also need to be educated on the difference between developmental and evaluative feedback. Developmental feedback (such as 360-degree feedback) is more subjective, and may reflect what the individual and her coach thinks about the progress being made toward achieving goals. Evaluative feedback is more related to performance appraisal and refers to more objective, measurable goals, such as sales volume, profit percentages and employee turnover.

Most developmental feedback should not be made public. It belongs to the individual, who shares it with others as he or she sees fit. The Individual Learning Plans that grows out of the feedback, however, should be shared with top management. In fact, individuals should be held accountable for achieving their Individual Learning Plans. In this way, the management team learns what action is taking place to move the company toward its leadership goals and can monitor individuals' personal development.

Sharing 360-degree and other individual feedback can hurt ones' ability to grow and change. It can lead to labeling people or reinforcing existing stereotypes about characteristics and capabilities. Individuals need time, space and support to work on their identified weaknesses and shore up their strengths. If appropriate, subsequent rounds of feedback can be more widely shared.

### Dilemma #2: How do family culture, communication and unity help or hinder the career development process?

Families that have the easiest time with career development are those where trust is high, communication is excellent and people love and are committed to helping one another no matter what their family position. Family members enjoy a high degree of unity, exemplified by their commitment to the business and their desire to see it succeed. They are not oriented towards promoting or protecting their favorite relatives but seek to uncover the greatest talent. They may realize that career development didn't happen in the previous generation, when sink-or-swim was the mentality, and that the family now wants to do things differently. They understand that both the family and the business have become much more complex. And, the family may have a history of stepping outside of what's comfortable or easy——after all, Mom and Dad took some big risks to start this business. That tradition of support for risk-taking will benefit the career-development effort. Families with such characteristics, background and foresight tend to embrace the career-development process and take right to it.

In families where the communication is indirect or highly emotional, people will have more trouble with an open, honest career-development process. In many such companies, family members protect weak relatives or are defensive about their performance. The directness and honesty required by a career-development process will be a big departure for these companies. Although it seems very threatening, it is in these companies that career development, carefully done, can make the most positive impact.

The best advice is to go slow, tread carefully, protect confidentiality and never use the data or the process in a negative or punitive manner. If the process is used as a means to punish or dismiss employees, or if employees are not given the chance to respond to their feedback, it will fail to develop future talent. Punitive processes can destroy what little trust exists.

**Dilemma #3: If you've never given honest feedback in the past, how do you start?**

Don't rush in. Planning and preparing the participants is essential. It may be necessary to hire a family business consultant to help your family build relationships and develop communication skills before starting the career-development process. In one case, it took a family a year and a half to build enough of a foundation of trust to successfully begin their 360-degree feedback process.

## Keep Things Fresh and Meaningful

Career development is not a race. There is no finish line. Allow the entire career-development process to unfold over time. Following a 360-degree feedback, a person can expect to work with a coach or engage in some other form of follow-up for at least 12 months. After that, new goals will be discussed and pursued. Real change takes time and because it does, individuals may lose energy or focus. It helps to mix things up and keep the process fresh. A boss or coach can suggest that the individual sign up for a one-day workshop out of the office or spend a half-day at home working on a development activity that he can't get to at the office. To provide fresh challenges, young managers should be given new assignments.

Employees should understand that career development is no mere exercise. It allows individuals to work on strengthening capacities truly important for the business. If the process is not viewed as meaningful, busy employees may too easily avoid career-development activities, like working on leadership skills, for pursuits that appear to be more "productive" or urgent. As important as it is for individuals to do their jobs, the organization must also insist upon their development work.

**EXHIBIT 5**

# The Career-Development Planning Process at a Glance

### 1. Create a picture of future leadership needs of the enterprise:

— Project into the future: How does the family define the company's values and vision?

— Project into the future: What changes do we expect inside and outside the company in the next 2-5 years?

— Project into the future: What key leadership competencies will the enterprise require?

### 2. Create a picture of current leadership in the enterprise.

— Identify high-potential future leaders. Include family and non-family.

— Assess their dreams and desires, education, competencies, skills, and experience. Consider using a 360-degree feedback.

— Assess the gap between current competencies and future needs.

### 3. Conduct a "gap analysis" and create individual career developments plans to bridge the gap.

— Each potential leader will create a learning plan based on his/her individual assessment.

— Each is assigned a mentor and a coach and meets regularly with both.

— Each actively pursues his/her individual career development.

### 4. Create accountability and follow-up.

— A "Continuity Task Force" meets regularly to review progress on career plans.

# VI. Maximizing Talent in a Family Business

In Chapter III we discussed the three stages of employment—Experimentation, Entry, and Expansion. Career development and the maximizing of one's talents are most concerned with the third stage, Expansion. By the time they have reached the Expansion stage, young leadership candidates have held summer jobs or internships in the family business, have gone to college, have several years' worth of outside work experience, and have moved successfully into responsible jobs in the family firm. They have committed themselves to making their career in the family business and to being on a track where they can eventually be considered for senior management positions and even, perhaps, for the CEO role.

Let's say your Expansion stage people are now well engaged in the career-development process described in the previous chapter. They have completed the 360-degree feedback process and have created their own Individual Learning Plans. How will you maximize their talent and help them develop into the future leaders that the business needs? A combination of on-the-job-training, coaching and mentoring and other techniques produce the best results.

## On-the-Job Training Regimens

Is it best to move potential leaders through a wide variety of departments, where they will get a broad but superficial exposure? Or is it better for them to spend 12-24 months in one area, really sinking their teeth into the work, developing deeper relationships and proving themselves more fully? The answer, of course, is "it depends." You will want them to spend time in areas where they can gain the knowledge and experience that best meets the company's future leadership needs. Those departments that will not move them toward their own or company goals will not be given as much attention.

Future leaders should get exposure to all key areas of the business including finance, human resources, sales and marketing, operations, information technology, strategic planning and new product development. During the Expansion stage, these employees should be in the field, in line rather than staff jobs. Real credibility will come with having some responsibility for your company's products or services. Potential leaders may avoid operational responsibility because it entails longer hours and less flexibility, and may be located "out in the sticks." Don't let them resist. Jobs in the field expose them to the core of what the company does.

At times, young managers may resist a "staff" position. They may not be drawn to accounting or feel comfortable in human resources. Experience in these functions, however is also crucial.

Be sensitive, to individual reactions. People needn't spend excessive time in jobs or locations that they detest. For example, a natural salesperson—someone who loves talking and visiting with other people—might feel like he is in purgatory if he is forced to spend too much time in finance. He may need to put in his time to prove credibility and learn the basics, but he doesn't need to stay so long that he becomes depressed. Alternatively, a less outgoing person who is drawn to numbers, and is very comfortable spending time in finance may need to be pushed to get out and learn to be more interactive and socialize with co-workers as a crucial leadership skill.

Career development means crafting plans to give leaders experience, but being prepared to change plans as the process moves forward.

You may be asking, "How much special treatment should a family member get? Do they get a job only when a bona fide opening exists? Or are positions created especially for them?" There are pros and cons to both approaches. Sticking too rigidly to one or the other approach causes problems. If, for example, a temporary job is created to facilitate for a family member's development, everyone needs to know that the purpose is to provide a young family member with specific experience. A similarly talented non-family person may be placed in a temporary position for development as well.

For insight into how one very successful business-owning family provided for maximizing the talents of potential family leaders, take a look at *The Trust: The Private and Powerful Family Behind* The New York Times," by Susan E. Tifft and Alex S. Jones. It describes in particular the rigorous training that the current CEO, Arthur Ochs Sulzberger Jr., underwent. When he was named publisher of the *Times*, say the authors, "he was the most thoroughly prepared publisher *The New York Times* had ever had."[6] You will see that even though this is the case, his career development process enjoyed dramatic twists and turns as it unfolded.

## "Development In Place"

"How much can I really learn and grow if I'm in the family business for most of my career?" That's a question young family members often ask. The answer is: that's up to you. You can learn a lot if you open your mind, even if you stay in the same job for a long period of time.

Researchers at the Center for Creative Leadership (CCL), in Greensboro, NC, suggests that you don't have to move around to get valuable learning opportunities. You can gain fresh experiences on your current job through a series of special assignments. CCL calls this "development in place." Some of the experiences that stretch a person include appointments to committees or task forces, responsibility for special projects, visits to clients, meetings with colleagues in other parts of the country or abroad, or starting something from scratch. One CCL report you might find useful is "Eighty-Eight Assignments for Development in Place." You will find CCL listed in the Resources section of this book.

## Coaches and Mentors

You will recall that as part of the career-development process, potential leaders often find or are assigned a coach and/or mentor. While both serve as instructors and trainers, there are some important differences between the two:

**1. A coach is a professional who is paid to help trainees identify and reach their development goals.** Coaching is a more formal process than mentoring.

**A successful family business coach must do a good job of being challenging and supportive at the same time.** An excellent coach holds a high level of expectations for the person being coached. She doesn't accept people's excuses without question. She pushes-and-prods and raises the bar. At the same time, she knows that the coaching process will work only if the trainee feels well supported. The coach needs to be an excellent listener. People will let down their guard and show their strengths and weaknesses only when they know the coach is on their side.

In essence, a coach helps you figure out where you are now, where you want to be, and what steps you must take to bridge the gap. The coaching process starts with an assessment of the trainee's capabilities and career goals and interests. The coach may also talk to people in the business and family who are important in the trainee's life to get a complete picture. Then the coach and trainee sit down together, talk about goals, and complete an Individual Learning Plan and lay out a time-frame for development.

Some coaching is very intensive, with the coach checking back with the trainee on a weekly basis to see if specific assignments were implemented or goals met. There will be discussions of why progress was made or not and how things are going, and a new set of goals may be established. Other coaches work on a less-intensive schedule, being in contact with the trainee every two weeks, monthly or even quarterly.

The logistics of coaching need to be considered. If the coach lives in another city, will coaching sessions take place primarily by telephone, with face-to-face meetings on an occasional basis? How often will the coach and trainee speak? Who will make the call? What kinds of notes are needed and what kind of follow-up should be expected? Who else should be involved in the process? Will the coach be asked to report to the trainee's parent or to a non-family executive about the progress? Who else is to be updated, and is that agreeable to everybody involved? Again, what rules of confidentiality should be observed?

Someone who works in your business can be considered as a coach, as long as they have the training and skills for the job. More likely, you will engage someone from outside. What is crucial is that the coach you hire has been previously successful working with family businesses and has the necessary understanding of the complexities of family business. To determine their qualifications, you will need to ask coaching candidates questions such as: Have you worked for other family businesses? How do you see family businesses as being different from non-family businesses? What do you see as the special opportunities and challenges in family businesses, and how do you address those in your coaching? Can you tell me about a time when you helped an employee in a family business untangle family and business issues?

Information about finding an appropriate coach can be found in the Resource section at the end of this book.

**2. A mentor is an older, more seasoned person who wants to share his or her experience with someone younger.** Mentors customarily are not paid for this role, and the process of mentoring is more informal than that of coaching. Meetings and discussions are more likely to take place on an as-needed basis, perhaps over lunch, during a round of golf, or by telephone or e-mail.

A mentor imparts wisdom and guidance to the younger person based upon their own personal experiences. A mentor is not necessarily a trained professional "helper." They serve more as a knowledgeable and concerned ally. The protégé might ask, "Here's a problem I'm faced with. How did you handle it when that happened to you?" And they'll have a conversation about the issue at hand.

Sometimes the mentor is an older family or non-family executive in the family business. Board members and loving family members can also be excellent sources of mentoring. What often works especially well, however, is to choose a mentor who is the CEO or a senior executive of another family company. At the Next-Generation Leadership Institute at Loyola University Chicago, the young participants are each assigned a mentor from another family business. This could be a CEO who has turned over the business to his son, or a non-family executive who was on hand when a business was passed on to the next generation.

Loyola University Chicago's Family Business Center is one of the top family business programs in the country. Its Next Generation Leadership Institute (NGLI) is an 18-month program specifically designed to prepare next generation leaders to lead their family business. NGLI was designed by a select group of family business leaders that was asked to design the career-development program they wished had been available when they were preparing themselves for family business leadership. Geared for men and women ranging in age from their late 20's to early 40's, NGLI provides monthly facilitated support groups called Peer Labs, comprehensive psychological assessments, individual coaching towards accomplishment of Individual Learning Plans and prominent leaders of successful family businesses serving as mentors. Many NGLI participants come to the program with MBA's from prominent universities, but are still seeking the personal development that will allow them to chart the rocky course of leading their family businesses. Participants include those working in the business as leaders as well as those not working in the business but providing leadership for family issues.

Research suggests that there are some advantages to having senior family members serve as mentors. They understand the culture and the values of the family, and they can give protégés the "inside scoop" that an outsider can't. The advantages of non-family mentors may be even more substantial. You generally get more objective feedback, especially if the mentor is from another business. If the process does not work out well, mentor and protégé can go their separate ways, but if the mentor is a family member and something emerges during the process that isn't favorable to the young person, it can hound him for the rest of his career. Additional distance that comes with having a non-family mentor can be very positive for younger people.[7]

Even though mentors don't get paid, they do get something in return for their efforts: the opportunity to see things through a younger person's eyes. Suppose the mentor is a senior member of another family business where younger family members are clamoring for leadership positions. By meeting intimately and regularly with a next-generation leader from another business, the mentor gains a great deal of insight on his own situation and his own children and the challenges they are experiencing.

## Other Sources of Help

Young people can take special courses and seminars, or even be given the opportunity to get an executive MBA on weekends. They can join peer groups, such as The Executive Committee (www.teconline.com) or the Young Presidents' Organization (www.ypo.org), which offer not only educational programs but also the opportunity to share experiences. If they are not eligible for membership in TEC or YPO, they can form peer groups of their own, or perhaps find one at a nearby university that has a family business center.

They can join industry or professional groups and attend conferences, having the opportunity to rub shoulders with more experienced, knowledgeable people or to sit in on educational sessions. Volunteer activities can be sought out that will provide experience to complement the experience that a young person is getting on the job. There is, it seems, almost no end of ways to maximize future leadership talent in a family firm.

**EXHIBIT 6**  ███████████████████████████████

## *11 Great Ways To Expand Your Skills and Knowledge*

1. Get experience in a variety of jobs in different departments.

2. Switch a staff job for line responsibilities.

3. Volunteer for special assignments at work.

4. Visit clients and vendors and learn from them.

6. Find a mentor.

7. Hire a coach.

8. Begin an executive MBA or other advanced degree.

9. Join industry or professional groups and attend their conferences and other educational programs.

10. Do volunteer work that offers challenges and useful experience.

11. Join a peer group that provides educational opportunities and a chance to share experiences with others.

# VII. Who's Responsible for What?

Nearly everyone plays a role in career development in a family business. Here is how those roles shape up:

The family serves as the guiding light. It provides the overall vision and values that frame the entire process. If the family holds a strong belief in work-life

*The family serves as the guiding light. It provides the overall vision and values that frame the entire process.*

balance, it might encourage family members to consider working part-time while their children are young. By contrast, another family might say, "Anyone who chooses to work part-time will never be seriously considered for a top management position." Another family might place great emphasis on community involvement, saying, "We expect our leaders to serve the community in some way." If so, voluntary activities would become a part of career development.

The family also establishes, hopefully in writing, the policies that govern employment and promotion of family members in the business.[8] An employment policy sets forth answers to such questions as: Do we always want to develop a family member as the CEO, or will we select the best person for the job, family member or not? Do we want to actively encourage the next generation to work in the business? What are our requirements for family members who want to join the business? What are our criteria for promoting family members? Shall we make internship opportunities available early on to kids, whether or not they're motivated to work in the business?

If a board of directors has been charged with the responsibility of choosing successors for the company's top leadership positions, family members need to resist lobbying the board. It's important that they accept and support the board's decisions, even when outcomes are not precisely what family members hoped for. If there's no board, a fair career-development process itself helps to lessen family politicking around promotion decisions. However, the family needs to agree to abide by the results of the process and to avoid behind-the-scenes maneuvering. It helps to devote time at family meetings to explain the career-development process so that family members fully understand and give it their full support.

**The board of directors** holds the company's top management accountable for defining competencies needed for the future and for making career and leadership development a priority. It supports management's efforts to devote adequate resources, time and attention to the process. It shows its commitment and intent by regularly asking about and discussing leadership and career development. Board members regularly check in on the topic with the CEO and other key executives by asking, "What are you doing about developing your successors?"

*The board of directors holds the company's top management accountable for defining competencies needed for the future and for making career and leadership development a priority.*

Where active boards exist, they have the final responsibility to select successors for key company positions. Board members can make it known that they want to interact with high-potential candidates who have the performance record, skills, knowledge and experience to fill future strategic needs. Indeed, presenting to the board is an outstanding developmental experience.

**The individual**—that is, the person whose career is the subject of development—is responsible for his or her own learning and growth. If that's you, it means pursuing development and growth through education, job experience, and community service—wherever you can find opportunities to stretch yourself. You must understand yourself, define your talents as you see them, think about what you really want and what makes you happy. Seek feedback and act on it. Be willing to try something new and be willing to change. Be open to the fact that you can change—even if you're 50 years old or more. It's never too late. Even if you get discouraged and upset, try to maintain a positive attitude. One family member became very discouraged by the feedback she received but she finally made the decision that she wanted to continue with the process. "I can do better and I want to do better," she said. She knew the responsibility was in her hands.

**The organization,** meaning top management in the family business, is responsible for initiating, designing and implementing a career-development process that will assure future leaders for the organization's needs. Top management may delegate the actual responsibility to someone else, such as a human resources director, but management is ultimately accountable for results. Management must define the key competencies called for by the company's strategic plan. They must make development and growth opportunities available and budget for them. Management makes sure that people get support for their education in terms of time and financial resources. Management also makes sure people are mentored and coached as needed. And, most important, management sets the bar by providing honest, constructive feedback to individuals who report to them.

*The organization is responsible for initiating, designing and implementing a career-development process that will assure future leaders for the organization's needs.*

EXHIBIT 7 █████████████████████████

# Who's Responsible for What In Career Development and Succession?

## Family

Shapes the beliefs and values it wants expressed by company leadership in pursuit of company strategy.

Determines the overall philosophy to guide a family employment policy.

Accepts and supports the board's final decisions regarding promotion decisions.

## Board of Directors

Approves the company's strategic plan and makes sure it defines future leadership needs.

Holds organization accountable for devoting resources and attention to the career development of future leaders.

Makes the ultimate selection of successors for key company positions, based on their achievements, skills, knowledge, and experience.

## Individual

Understands self. Defines personal talents, skills and career goals and desires.

Pursues development and growth opportunities.

Seeks and responds to feedback.

## Organization

Defines company strategy and goals. Identifies key competencies needed for future.

Makes development and growth opportunities available to individuals.

Requires that honest, constructive performance feedback is given to individuals.

## The Role of Non-Family Executives

The support of non-family executives is essential to successful career development in family businesses. In many family businesses, family members are expected to hold top positions. In these cases, non-family managers must understand and accept with grace the fact that they will never be CEO. They must truly be devoted to the development of the next-generation of family members. These non-family executives are to be prized and shown appreciation by the family. The teaching they offer and the feedback they give to young family members reflects incomparable generosity. Reward such non-family executives well.

*The support of non-family executives is essential to successful career development in family businesses.*

41

Be aware, however, that this kind of support for career development is not always present—particularly when it comes to preparing family members for future leadership. A non-family manager may not have his or her heart fully engaged in the process of bringing young family members along in their careers. Often such non-family managers cling to an ill-founded belief that they will one day be CEO, no matter how clear the family thinks it has made themselves that only a family member will hold the top position. When non-family executives nurture this illusion, they may sabotage the development of high-potential next-generation family members. They may assign family members to tasks beyond current abilities or withhold support or information needed for success. Non-family managers also have been known to foster dissent or gossip worrying parents unnecessarily.

Be clear with non-family executives when the family has set a goal of keeping family members in the top spot. Be prepared to take action if a non-family manager doesn't "get it" and, as a result, undermines the career-development process.

**EXHIBIT 8** ▐▬▬▬▬▬▬▬▬▬▬▬▬▬▬▬▬▬▬

## *Helping or Hindering Career Development*

**Non-family executives help when they...**

... understand when they themselves will not become CEO. In fact, they may prefer a key supporting role.

... enthusiastically embrace the important role of helping next-generation family members prepare for leadership positions.

... serve as coaches or mentors.

... provide appropriate learning and development experiences for young family members.

... offer encouragement and emotional support to their charges.

... enjoy the success of their protégés.

**Non-family executives hinder when they...**

... mistakenly assume they have a shot at being CEO.

... fail to understand their role in developing next-generation family members.

... sabotage young family members by giving them assignments that are far beyond them or keeping them out of the information loop.

... deny young family members emotional support and encouragement.

... worry parents or board members unnecessarily about their offspring.

## Show Them the Money

Preparing future leaders has its costs and one of the organization's responsibilities is to budget for career development.

You'll need to think about paying for courses, conferences, workshops and seminars for tomorrow's executives. Perhaps you'll want to send someone for an advanced degree, or hire a coach to work with younger family members. You may need to pay for travel to other locations for experience or educational opportunities. Dues for memberships in associations or other organizations may be required.

In short, career development should be part of the company's budget. Be careful not to create a false economy. If you haven't spent your budget in this crucial area, the chances are that the job is not being done. Everyone should realize that these expenses are part of the cost of doing business. More important, the family business's willingness to budget for career development demonstrates how important it regards the process and how committed to it the family and the business are.

As you see the process unfold and family members develop their skills and abilities, you and others in your family will begin to feel immense pride and satisfaction. You will witness your children, nieces and nephews demonstrating new levels of competence. And you will know that you are taking the steps needed to assure that your business survives and transitions into the next generation.

# VIII. Translating Career Development Into Promotion Decisions

Over time, as individuals gain experience and skills, the career-development process influences company promotion decisions. At this point, the processes of performance appraisals and career development interact. As a family business grows and develops it usually becomes more formal in its performance appraisal approach. It evolves from occasional informal conversations, to a strictly scheduled and highly structured process that is directly associated with salary increases. Even when businesses recognize the need to become more organized about performance appraisal, giving employees clear feedback about how they are doing; family businesses rarely include family members in that process. It is just too awkward for parents to evaluate their children or siblings to evaluate each other. The whole process is too often ignored or bypassed. As a result, discomfort is avoided but so are the important benefits of giving and receiving constructive performance feedback. Performance appraisal is vital to leadership development and must eventually interface with career development.

As we discussed earlier, best practice dictates that career development and performance appraisal be kept separate. The processes are very different. Development is about helping people grow and change. That requires honesty, vulnerability and risk. "Here are skills and abilities you need to strengthen." "You need to understand marketing more fully." Performance appraisal is about evaluation: how well did people perform against expectations? "Here's where you're doing well and here's where you're falling short." "You did a great job with that new product." "You haven't met your sales goals."

It can also help to separate career development and the performance appraisal in time. Many companies hold development conversations in the spring and performance appraisals in the fall. This separation can be especially important when potential leaders are still in the early stages of development, when they may be more vulnerable to criticism, but when they may be more malleable and responsive to feedback.

You will recall that in Chapter V, we recommended keeping the first round of career-development feedback confidential. Then, second or third rounds of assessment could be shared as needed, as long as everyone involved understands and agrees in advance. The information obtained in the career-development and performance appraisal processes should be recognized as very different. Regard them as two separate "buckets" of information used each for their own purpose. In other words, don't make performance appraisal decisions based on career-development feedback.

*Performance appraisal is vital to leadership development and must eventually interface with career development.*

45

## The Performance Management Cycle

It helps to think of the performance management cycle as a clock:

**EXHIBIT 9** ████████████████████████████████████

### *The Performance Management Cycle*

**Performance Goals**

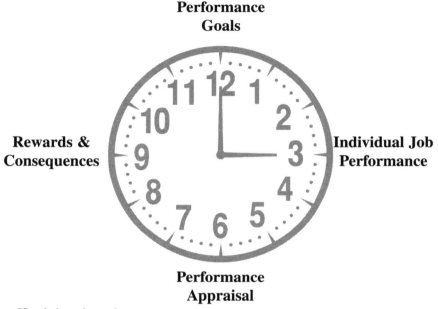

**Rewards & Consequences**

**Individual Job Performance**

**Performance Appraisal**

Here's how it works:

**1. Performance Goals.** At the outset, at 12 o'clock, the employee receives clear performance goals. These might be defined by the individual, by their supervisors or by the board. However it's done, **clear goal setting is essential. No one at any level can perform to expectations if they don't know what the expectations are. Employees have to know what they are being measured against.**

**2. Performance.** People perform their jobs and management maintains awareness on how the work is being done.

**3. Measurement.** At 6 o'clock, the annual performance appraisal takes place. The individual receives constructive feedback about how he or she performed against goals and expectations.

**4. Rewards and Consequences.** At 9 o'clock, the results of the assessment are communicated. Depending on how they performed, employees are promoted, given raises, put on probation, scheduled for specific training, or perhaps demoted or dismissed. At this time, the goals may also re-evaluated and adjusted.

**Goals are meaningless without feedback and consequences. At the same time, consequences without clear goals set in advance provide little value for your employee. Family businesses can be especially vulnerable to these dangers because of the awkward nature of giving feedback to a relative.**

## So Simple But So Hard to Do

As you can see, the concept is very simple: goal setting, performance, measurement and consequences. In practice, it's difficult to do. Performance appraisals aren't fun, especially if you have to give negative feedback. It's even worse if you have to fire someone, demote them or take other action that may be good for the business but hurt or anger individuals. Sometimes you may feel constrained from taking needed action because you risk the wrath of family members or shareholders.

The key is to be honest in a kind and constructive way. Keep the focus on the job, not the individual. Talk about performance, not opinion. Give examples and provide both positive and corrective feedback. Approach performance appraisals with compassion and caring but without denying the need to confront performance problems.

## Difficult Decisions Emerge

By creating an employment policy in advance and by integrating a planned career-development process with a performance management system, you can begin to tackle some of your most difficult situations—the uncle who is a chronic performance problem, the cousin who did poorly the first time around as an employee and who now wants another chance, the aunt who wants a promotion for her son, and so on. The process is clear to everyone, as are performance expectations. All will see that there is a fair and objective process for developing potential leaders. Some people will weed themselves out. The career-development process may help them see that being a CEO or operations vice president is not for them and that they would much rather be doing research or directing design.

Others may have to be weeded out. For some, being a part of the family means having a leadership job in the family business. But what if they aren't capable? They need to be directed as kindly as possible to jobs where their talents can shine, either in the family business or elsewhere. In the short term, they may be unhappy. But, if you're lucky, they'll thank you later for deterring them from a career choice that would have made them frustrated and miserable. They may say something like, "Uncle Marcus, remember when you said I wasn't going to be promoted to vice president and you advised me to go back to the finance department? I was really mad at first, but it's one of the best things that ever happened to me. I love working with numbers and I'm really good at it. I've had a wonderful career and I feel I've made important contributions to this company."

As career development and performance management work together, it will become clearer and clearer which next-generation leaders have what it takes to become CEO of your family business. If more than one such leader emerges, you'll have some options. In some family businesses the current CEO chooses his or her successor. Others expect the final decision to be made by the board of directors. That relieves family members of having to make difficult decisions about one another and helps preserve family harmony. A board can make the choice more objectively, gathering data and establishing criteria for the selection. The family, however, has to agree in advance to accept the board's decision. Some families are reluctant to relinquish the succession selection to a board.

Still another possibility is to create co-CEOs or put leadership in the hands of a talented sibling or cousin team. More and more family businesses are trying this kind of team leadership.[9]

Whatever you do, a career-development process lets you know that your family and your company have fulfilled their responsibility to develop talent to meet the future leadership needs of the business.

*A career-development process lets you know that your family and your company have fulfilled their responsibility to develop talent to meet the future leadership needs of the business.*

# IX. Family Leaders Need Development, Too

What if you own stock but don't work in the business? Then your task is to be an effective owner of the business. That's an important responsibility in itself. It becomes even more important when you take on leadership responsibilities, such as service on the family business's board of directors, being an officer of a family council or committee, or becoming involved in community service.

You wouldn't think of having a business without a leader, but too often, business-owning families don't think about the need for a *family* leader. The role is often filled in an unconscious, informal way. Frequently, it falls to Mom or Grandma. Unfortunately, it's often a behind-the-scenes, invisible, indirect, and even thankless role.

In some cases, the family business CEO realizes that the greatest potential danger to the business is conflict within the family shareholder group. Family shareholders may not understand their roles and responsibilities as owners. The shareholder group, disorganized, leaderless and without a clear set of goals and direction can become contentious or irresponsible about their ownership, threatening the stability of the business.[10] The CEO may begin to think of ways to develop family leadership, perhaps seeing to it that there's a family reunion or other gathering once a year, paid for by the company as a shareholder relations expense.

**A far better way is for the family to agree that family leadership is needed, plan for it in an organized, strategic way and give it the respect and recognition it deserves.** As you will see from "One Family Leader's Story" below, some family leaders are so valued that they are compensated for their important work.

## What Do Family Leaders Do?

In essence, a family leader promotes the unity, understanding and harmony of current family members, but in order to keep the family strong and to support the success of the business and its transition to the next generation of family owners. Depending on the size of the family, the number of family shareholders, the family talent available and other factors, family leadership is carried out in a number of different ways. One person might informally emerge, or more rarely be designated, as THE family leader. In other cases, several people share the role. In some families, a variety of leadership positions are created: chair of a family council, chair or CEO of a family foundation, chairs of specific committees, and the like. These positions often rotate so that everyone is engaged and involved.

Some of the possible functions of family leaders include:

**Serve as family representative to the board of directors, representing owners' interests and concerns on the board.**

**Plan family meetings.** Set the agenda, plan the logistics and serve as liaison with the facilitator.

**Organize family events.** This might include a family picture, a holiday outing, a family vacation, or organizing meals for those in need or doing some other community service as a group.

**Taking the pulse of the family and promoting informal and formal communication.** This fosters knowledge about important developments in the family and in the business. It may include editing a regular family newsletter or maintaining a secure family web site. This allows the family to stay in touch with each other and with the business CEO/President.

**Serve as the "family glue."** See to relationship building, maintenance and repair; listen to the soft-spoken; arrange for the integration of new family members into the family and provide emotional family leadership in other ways as needed.

**Provide the next generation with a solid foundation of values, security, love and affection**—a traditional but very necessary role.

Now and then, a truly wise and powerful family leader emerges. One such family leader was Iphigene Sulzberger, matriarch of the family that has controlling ownership of The New York Times Co. While her husband, Arthur Hays Sulzberger, the CEO, was still alive, she usually deferred to him. However, after the premature death of their son-in-law, Iphigene and her daughters persuaded Arthur to name his son as successor. After Arthur's death, Iphigene came into her own. She served as a confidante to her son, Arthur Ochs Sulzberger, and it is said that he never made a major decision without consulting her. Just as important, she passed on values of family unity and reverence for *The New York Times* to the next generation inspiring them to put the good of the family and the newspaper ahead of personal desires. Her leadership served both the family and the business well.

## Pros and Cons

There are many pluses to designating official family leaders. Doing so relieves the business CEO of the burden of family leadership. Because the responsibilities of being a CEO are so demanding, it's almost impossible for the business leader to give sufficient focus to the family side of family business. Family leaders can step in and make sure that family and ownership issues receive adequate attention and resources. In many respects, the business CEO and the family leader act as partners so that the family can support the business and the business can support the family.

*The business CEO and the family leader act as partners so that the family can support the business and the business can support the family.*

Family leadership also gives family members not working in the business an opportunity to play meaningful roles. Family members who work in the business receive a great deal of satisfaction from their involvement.

50

When other family members take on family leadership responsibilities, they also get a chance to contribute their talents to the family enterprise, thus having their own chance to shine.

It makes sense to provide rewards and recognition for family leaders. A salary or other monetary compensation can be in order. For someone who plans the family meeting, an extra day at the resort, prior to the start of the meeting, might combine a treat with necessary preparation.

But there are some down sides to consider, too. In the founding generation, it's fairly easy for Mom and Dad to provide family leadership because they have the natural authority of their role as parents. But asserting family leadership becomes more difficult in the sibling and cousin generations. When individual family members step forward with the willingness, desire and talent to provide family leadership, they can draw the disapproval of their family peers. As a family member begins to take on more leadership in the family, others may view their actions with suspicion or mistrust. For example, something as innocent as volunteering to set a date and choose a location for a family meeting might be interpreted as controlling. The family might ask: "who put you in charge?" Nobody really minds when it's Mom and Dad or a venerated aunt or uncle takes initiative, but when it's a brother or a sister, things can get touchy. Siblings start asking questions like: "Why should you set the agenda?" "Why should you choose the place?" and, "Why should I stretch for you?"

Another danger is that if someone has a leadership role, other family members stand back and do less. They may feel relieved of the need to take responsibility, or may say, "We've asked him to be the family leader. Why is he asking what we think? He should make the decisions." Sometimes naming one person as the official leader results in other family members becoming more passive and disconnected. Obviously, maintaining the involvement of other family members is a real leadership challenge.

Is it better to rotate positions of family leadership or keep one person in the role more permanently? Obviously, there are pros and cons to each approach. Rotating positions has the advantage of involving a greater number of people. It spreads out responsibilities. It requires everyone to be involved at some point and gives everyone a chance to grow their skills. On the con side however, everyone may not have the skill, ability or interest to hold a family leadership position. Insisting that they fill a role under these circumstances can be damaging to the individual and the family. As always, each family has to find their own approach to family leadership. One answer will not fit all.

## Preparing for Family Leadership

While family leaders historically have tended to emerge in an informal, unplanned way, families can plan and develop leadership for the family as they do for the business. The approach your family takes will depend on the size and complexity of your family and business and the family structures you create. Do you have a family council? Are there committees? Do you have regular shareholder and family meetings? Is there a family foundation? All of these require leadership.

Your family can use many of the development ideas suggested in earlier chapters. Keep in mind that it's just as important to establish a fair process for leadership development on the family side as it is in the business.

How can family leaders be developed and where will they come from? Involvement of the next generation, as described in Chapter IV is the place to start. Continued ownership education is essential as children become teenagers and young adults. So are internships in the business that help them develop an understanding of and appreciation of their legacy. By their late teens and early twenties, next generation family members can begin to take on committee assignments. You can watch their progress and see to it that they are mentored for more responsible roles and given feedback on their performance. As they mature, they can gain experience as a committee chair. They can move up through the ranks of the family council, starting as treasurer and then becoming secretary, vice president, and president.

Just as outside experience is helpful to family members who wish to join the family firm, experience outside the family is helpful to those who aspire to family leadership. Volunteer work, especially that which leads to greater and greater responsibility, is a good training ground for family leadership. Suppose your son has worked long and hard as a volunteer for the community art museum and has now been invited to sit on its board and serve as chairman of its strategic planning committee. Obviously he has developed many capacities that will translate well into a family leadership role.

Watch how younger family members' careers develop and assess them for potential. Take Kirsten, who started out as an elementary school teacher, has been promoted to assistant principal and then principal; she has skills the family should be eager to tap. Or Angelo, who has been named assistant city manager of a small but thriving municipality. It's clear that his colleagues have confidence in his abilities and that he would bring great value to the family's leadership needs as well.

As long as they are committed to the family and the business, family leaders can come from a variety of disciplines and experiences. Here is one example:

## One Family Leader's Story

Sarah Schmidt knows just how hard and, at the same time, how exhilarating and rewarding family leadership can be—because she has emerged as a leader of the Schmidt family, which owns U.S. Oil Co., Inc., in Combined Locks, WI. A member of the business family's third generation, Sarah has just assumed a position on the company's board. She previously was chairperson of the Executive Committee of the family's Owners Council. As such she represented one of the three branches of the family, and the two cousins who served on the Executive Committee with her represent the family's other two branches.

"If you want a healthy family business," she says, "then you need to devote the time and the resources to developing a healthy family."

With 750 employees and around $1 billion in annual revenues, U.S. Oil engages in wholesale distribution, petroleum-related construction and reclamation, and retail convenience stores. Nearly 70 family members own shares in the company, and it's part of the family's culture to make even the youngest children shareholders. About 12 family members sit on the Owners Council, which monitors the strategic direction and performance of the company, assures that there's appropriate succession planning for both company and family leadership, and educates family members about the responsibilities and privileges of ownership.

The role of the Executive Committee is a particularly strong one because it serves as the company's board nominating committee and provides oversight to the board. It also handles family issues related to ownership. In recent years, it has put together a shareholder agreement and restructured U.S. Oil's board to have more independent directors than family members.

Sarah, had previously left a seat on the board to chair the Owners Council Executive Committee, points out that the Schmidt clan feels that the family responsibilities are just as important as the work of the board. The Executive Committee members are compensated for their time just as the board members are compensated. Sarah, who is in her early 30s and lives in Evanston, Il, estimates that she spends a day-and-a-half each week working on Executive Committee matters. Sarah has also sought to share her learning and the growth of her family with other family businesses through her involvement in Loyola University Chicago Family Business Center. She serves on the Center's board of directors and has presented to the membership on the accomplishments of her family and their council.

How is it that she developed into a family leader?

As she was growing up, Sarah took great pride in the family business. But she was resigned to the idea that she would not become involved in it because her interests lay elsewhere—in human relations, group dynamics and communications, not oil or accounting. She earned a degree in sociology and women's studies and a master's degree in counseling.

When she was about 25, she realized that the business was her major asset and that she needed, somehow, to be involved with it. Not long after, the Schmidts hired a family business consultant, who suggested that they create a family council. The Schmidts were excited about the concept and, recalls Sarah, "I was deemed the person to head up the task force to get a council formed."

Through the process of creating the Family Council (now the Owners Council), Sarah learned that there was such a field as family business and that there were resources to help families like hers. And, she says, she was excited to realize that the skills she had been developing in psychology, group dynamics, team building, leadership development and education "meshed beautifully with this really phenomenal business and really tremendous family."

Once she took seriously the prospect of being involved in the business from the family side, she began to educate herself, attending seminars, workshops and conferences on family business. She sought out people who were in the field of family business or who held roles similar to hers in other business-owning families. She also enrolled in the Next Generation Leadership Institute at the Loyola University Chicago Family Business Center. The learning process, she says with a chuckle, has also "meant buying more bookshelves to house my family business library."

Being a family leader isn't easy, however. For example, Sarah and her father, who is now retired, made the painful discovery that they disagreed on a number of important issues.

*"It's my job to bring the business closer to the shareholders and to do that through education and communication,"*

"I really learned a lot about being my own person and what it means to be an adult in the world and making your own decisions and being responsible and accountable for those decisions," she says. "But the reality of disagreeing with my dad and not always being on his side was really a huge test for our relationship."

Sarah says she "had no clue" that being a family leader would require as much courage as it sometimes does. "I thought it was going to just be so much fun! In all the other positions I've had, where I've been working with building teams and doing leadership development work, I never encountered challenges like this, but I also never really was stretched as much either."

Early life experiences that helped develop her as a family leader included summer jobs in the family business. She spent one summer filing, another cleaning test tubes in a company lab, and still another washing windshields and stocking shelves in one of the convenience centers.

As this book goes to press, Sarah, now a family business consultant, is completing a doctorate in clinical psychology. Her own experience has taught her that family leaders need to be "great communicators" and to be politically savvy--understanding family dynamics, connecting with people, and building alliances.

Equally important is setting the example of what an effective owner is. "Whenever I'm making a decision, I'm always aware that what's good for me personally might be totally different than what's good for the whole shareholder group." Sometimes, she has to vote against her own best interest and go with the best decision for the family.

Her advice to other business families is to take the family-leadership roles seriously by defining the roles, seeking out people who want the responsibility, holding them accountable, and paying them for their time.

"It's my job to bring the business closer to the shareholders and to do that through education and communication," Sarah says. As a result of leadership on the family side, she points out, family members show enormous enthusiasm for and interest in the business. That makes it easier to make decisions more quickly and to meet the challenges of owning a business.

**EXHIBIT 10** ▰▰▰▰▰▰▰▰▰▰▰▰▰▰▰▰▰▰▰▰

# *Great Family Leaders ...*

... build trust with everyone.

... have excellent communication skills.

... make sure everyone in the family is heard, even the shy and quiet ones.

... serve as a role model to other family members on what it means to be an effective owner.

... help younger family members prepare for and find their place in the family experience.

... keep in touch with family members and with the business CEO.

... transmit the family's values to the younger generations.

... educate themselves about family business and educate other family members.

... possess the ability and willingness to be a mediator or negotiator and to bridge different points of view.

... focus family members on what unites them.

... get along well with family members of all ages.

... have courage. They may have to disagree with or make decisions that disappoint other family members.

... are passionate about their family and their business.

# X. Where Families Falter

A business-owning family can experience a number of common pitfalls in the career-development process. If you are mindful of them, you can take action to avoid these familiar traps. Any one of them can sabotage your career-development efforts.

**Lack of commitment to career development.** For reasons discussed in Chapter II, many families cannot bring themselves to initiate and stand behind a career-development program. Others may launch an effort but let it falter as they fail to provide necessary support and resources. They may stint on the mentors and coaches, forget to insure that young people get new challenges and work experiences to help them grow, or fail to offer educational opportunities.

Families that lack commitment need to explore what is holding them back and find a way to overcome their roadblocks. Perhaps they feel that "everything is fine" right now and there's no need to rock the boat. If they let the effort drift away, they stand to fail the next generation on their road to leadership and endanger the business's future. The solution: clearly assign responsibility for the process and hold people accountable. Consider getting professional help in the form of a family business consultant.

**Poor communication skills.** In many families, it's tough to be honest in constructive ways. The family may feel it's not safe to expose their own needs and wants, they may worry about hurting other people's feelings, or they may fear someone else's anger. If family members can't communicate with one another effectively, it will be difficult, if not impossible, for them to establish and maintain a viable career-development process. Wise families may start by helping family members improve basic communication skills, then work on sessions at family meetings or workshops at conferences or university family business centers. In some cases, families may need to bring in professional help, such as a family therapist or psychologist with family business experience.[11]

**A "branch" mentality.** Too often, business families organize themselves into branches instead of thinking of themselves as one family. There's Harold's branch and Ashley's branch and Guy's branch and April's branch, and each sibling vies for what's best for the members of his or her own branch and so do their children and grandchildren.

How much better it is for family members to get past a branch mentality and think of what's best for the whole family and for the continued success of the business. Consider the recommendation made earlier in this book to provide equal access to summer jobs and internships for all children, not just the children of family members who work in the business. That's an example of doing what's best for the whole family because it gives all the young people the same opportunity. It's also good for the business because the company will have a larger talent pool from which to draw. Ultimately, all in the family will benefit.

**Politicking in the family.** A family with a branch mentality is particularly susceptible to politicking, but politicking can occur in any family. Politicking subverts career development by subverting open, fair processes. When a family member campaigns for a plum position for himself or for a son or daughter, he is sidestepping rules set up to assure that key jobs are awarded on ability and performance. If his attempt is successful, tension in the family will build, and the business itself may suffer because the best person for the job was not promoted. Some of the most successful business families educate their members about the dangers of politicking and create a culture that makes it clear that politicking is not condoned.

**Violating family business policies.** Family business consultants frequently advise families to create policies that set forth the rules for addressing issues such as family employment, decision making, governance and compensation. But sometimes families don't stick to the policies they create. In one typical scenario, the family agrees to an employment policy that states that "members of the next generation have to work outside the business for three years before they join the family firm." A son, as required, gets a job at another company. He works there just a year when Dad becomes convinced that he has to have the son back in the company. "It'll be best for him and it'll be best for the business," Dad says. He convinces the son to come back and the son does so, cutting off his opportunity to learn somewhere else before committing to the family business. And, just as bad, the policy has been undermined by those charged with upholding it.

In another common situation, a daughter, who did poorly in the family business and left two years ago, wants to return. However, the employment policy states that, "If a family employee leaves the business, he or she must wait five years before being considered for re-employment." The policy was intended to give young family members time to mature and to test their commitment before they are permitted to return. Nevertheless, the CEO dotes on his daughter and welcomes her return, even though she may not be ready.

It may be impossible to deter family members when they are bent on violating family policies. As a whole, however, families must make every attempt to stick to their policies. They were, after all, created to avoid problems in the first place.

**Lack of trust among family members.** When it is open and fair, a career-development process itself can help a family build trust. Nevertheless, families have to have enough trust initially to agree to setting up the process. Otherwise, they can't commit themselves to take the risks they think career development presents.

The process itself requires trust. A 360-degree exercise won't be effective unless family members and others involved trust each other enough to give and accept feedback.

If trust problems are not severe, a family can call in a professional facilitator to guide family members through some trust-building exercises. If trust is a

*One way to provide accountability is to create a board of directors with competent, knowledgeable outsiders on it.*

major issue, engaging a family therapist with family business experience may be the best solution.

**Failure to provide for family business accountability.** Providing accountability means setting up structures and systems to help assure that people are held responsible for their performance. One way to provide accountability is to create a board of directors with competent, knowledgeable outsiders on it. Such a board can evaluate the performance of the CEO, give feedback, make sure that management's actions are appropriate and honest, and in other ways assure that the company is operating at an optimum level. Another way is to set up career development and performance management systems and follow them through. In one classic accountability system, management by objectives (MBO), a goal and a timetable are set. Accountability for achieving that goal within the timeframe must be realized.

All too frequently, however, accountability is lacking in family businesses. The MBO process may lack sufficient follow up to make sure goals are achieved. Or the structures created permit too much conflict of interest to produce accountability. Suppose, three brothers are co-presidents of their family business. They are also major shareholders, and they, along with their mother, their spouses, and their sister comprise the board. How will the co-presidents be held accountable?

Most family business owners don't wish to be put in a position where they are evaluated by somebody else, so they shun the notion of having and compensating outside directors. Some of the most successful family business CEOs, however, welcome being held accountable. They know, that a board of directors can help them improve their performance and do a better job of running their company. They also understand that when accountability is present at the highest company levels, it filters down through the whole company, encouraging everyone to learn and grow and improve their own performance.

**Lack of respect for different skill sets and styles.** A hard-driving founder, used to giving orders and having them followed, may be mystified by and derisive of a son's attempt to "empower" people. The son, in turn, may despise his father's "command and control" approach. A "techie" may sneer at his cousin's technophobia, while that cousin worries about the loss of human touch in the company. Each, in his or her way, is right. Each has something to offer. What's best is if they recognize each other's strengths and contributions to the business, and understand that there are many ways to lead. One experienced manager put an almost opposite kind of leader in charge of an important project. He was shy and quiet while she was autocratic and demanding. But, she said, "Things always get better under his leadership." She knew his style didn't have to be like hers to manage well.

**Discouragement about or loss of energy for the career-development process.** Backslides are to be expected and, fortunately, you can anticipate them and plan for them. Some people get demoralized when they receive negative feedback. Shirley, the vice president of a third-generation chain of convenience stores was really crushed when her 360-degree feedback criticized her as being too demanding, too "hands-on." Until then, she had believed her people appreciated her management style and thought of her has being an involved manager striving for success. Instead, what they told her was, "We want you to back off some and let us do our jobs." Shirley thought about leaving the company but before she made a final decision, she let what she learned sink in. What she discovered was that she was strong on goals and vision but not so strong team-building and delegation. Before long, Shirley became reinvigorated and re-engaged. "I can do this," she said. "Let's build on my strengths and shore up my weaknesses."

Sometimes people just tire of the process and lose focus. This is frequently the case when company is doing well and dealing with the future seems unnecessary. "High water covers lots of stumps," said the leaders of one successful family business while allowing future potential problems to take care of themselves. Instead of easing up, the family needs to recommit itself and push even harder. See "Keep Things Fresh and Meaningful" in Chapter V for ideas on combating a dip in energy.

# XI. Summary

Career development is essential to the continuity of any family business. If a business is to survive, it has to have the leaders it needs for future success. But career development doesn't happen on its own. Owners, managers, board members and individuals themselves have to make it happen. In particular, if you are the CEO, you are responsible for the development of tomorrow's leaders. You may, of course, delegate the responsibility to others, but in the end, it's up to you to make sure the job gets done.

Family members may resist instituting a career-development program for a variety of reasons. They know it will require being honest with one another about professional shortcomings and they may fear hurting one another or damaging relationships. However, for the good of the business and, in turn, the long-range good of the family, such resistance must be overcome. Family members become more accepting of the career-development process when they see that it is open, fair and objective. It helps, too, if the family creates policies that sets forth the rules and expectations for employment and promotion of family members in the business. In some cases, a successful career-development process might initially require bringing in a professional consultant to help family members build trust and improve their communication with one another.

There are three stages of family employment: (1) Experimentation, in which children, teenagers, and college students learn the basics of the business through summer jobs and internships; (2) Entry, in which young people, after going to college and getting outside work experience, join the family business in their first "real" job; and (3) Expansion, when young family members finally commit their work lives to the family business and need the learning and development opportunities that will help them realize their fullest potential.

Smart families understand the importance of the first stage in generating young people's interest in and enthusiasm for the family's business. They know if young family members aren't excited enough to join the business, there won't be any family candidates for eventual career development. Such families often create a "Next-Generation Involvement Program" to teach children about the business from an early age and see to it that part-time jobs and internships are available to all young people in the family. A Next-Generation Involvement Program instills love for and commitment to the business and serves as a precursor to career development.

Serious, planned career development kicks in during the Expansion stage. It involves a four stage process that includes (1) envisioning future leadership needs; (2) doing a "gap analysis" by assessing current leadership competencies and comparing them with future needs; (3) having individuals plan and pursue their own growth and development with an eye toward closing the leadership gap, and (4) re-assessing, celebrating improvement, and planning the next cycle of development. Business families demonstrate their commitment to career development by budgeting sufficiently for it. They strengthen the accountability of the process by seeing to it that managers who take developing their people seriously and do it well get recognized and rewarded.

Families need to address several important issues with regard to career development. One is whether or not key leadership positions are open to all talented employees or just to qualified family members. Another is how much individual feedback should be confidential, when and with whom it may be shared, and how such information is to be used. Everyone involved needs to know what the rules are at the beginning of the process.

The career-development process exists side by side with, but is not the same as, performance appraisal. Career development is meant to encourage growth and learning and to provide a safe haven where young family members can be vulnerable and test themselves without fear of judgment. Performance appraisal is evaluative and judgmental. It is part of a performance management cycle that includes setting clear goals, performing, having one's performance measured against the goals, and consequences, which can mean rewards for good performance (promotions, raises) or penalties for falling short (lateral move to another job, demotion or dismissal)

Although they are somewhat interdependent, career development and performance appraisal should be kept as separate as possible. Feedback information gained about an individual in the career-development process should not be a basis for performance appraisal. It also helps to have career-development discussions with an individual at one time of year and performance appraisal at another.

In time, the most qualified leadership candidates emerge and selections for specific positions must be made, including that of CEO. Sometimes management, with the family's input and blessing, makes these decisions. When the company has an active board of directors, they may select the key leaders. Doing so results in more impartial, objective decisions and relieves the family of having to make decisions about family members that can cause lasting harm to relationships. The family must agree, however, to accept and abide by the board's decisions.

There will no doubt be some disappointments as a result of this process. Some family members may not get the jobs they were hoping for. Some parents may be unhappy that a son or daughter was not named CEO. But they will be better able to cope with their disappointment if they see that the processes for career development and leadership selection have been open, objective, impartial and fair.

A well-planned, effective career-development process creates a win-win opportunity for business-owning families. It enables individuals to grow in ways that meet their desires and abilities, and the business gains the talented leadership pool it needs to meet the strategic challenges of the future.

# Resources

## Human Resources and Leadership Tools
Center for Creative Leadership, One Leadership Place, P.O. Box 26300, Greensboro, North Carolina 27438-6300; (336)545-2810 or http://www.ccl.org.

Management Research Group, 14 York Street, Suite 301, Portland, Maine 04101; (207) 775-2173, or www.mrg.com

## Information and Referrals
The Family Firm Institute, a Boston-based organization of family business professionals, can be helpful in finding a coach. In Europe and other parts of the world, the association of family companies known as the Family Business Network can also help.

The Family Business Consulting Group Inc.<sup>sm</sup>, wants to insure that family businesses prosper. They are committed to forming long-term, professional relationships that explore solutions to family and business issues, decide on the best course of action and implement plans that will help the family business succeed for generations. You may contact them to help find you the appropriate professional.

Family Firm Institute, 200 Lincoln Street, #201, Boston, Massachusetts 02111; (617) 482-3049 or www.ffi.org

Family Business Network, P.O. Box 915, 23 Chemin de Bellerive, Lausanne Ch-1001, Switzerland; 41 21 618-0223 or http://www.fbn-i.org.

The Family Business Consulting Group, Inc.<sup>sm</sup>, 1220-B Kennesaw Circle, Marietta, Georgia 30066; 888-421-0110 or http://www.efamilybusiness.com.

## Education for Future Leaders
Next Generation Leadership Institute, Loyola University Chicago Family Business Center, 820 N. Michigan Avenue, Suite 1416, Chicago, Illinois, 60611; (312) 915-6490 or http://www.sb.luc.edu/centers/fbc.

## Education for Children
Business Cents Resources, 3038 Washington Pike, Bridgeville, Pennsylvania 15017; (412) 221-8122.

## Peer Groups
Young Presidents' Organization, Attn: Global Services Center, 451 S. Decker Drive, Irving, Texas 75062; (972) 650-4600 or http://www.ypo.org.

TEC International Headquarters, 5469 Kearny Villa Road, San Diego, California, 92123; 900-274-2367 or http://www.teconline.com.

# *Suggested Additional Readings*

Buckingham, Marcus and Coffman, Curt. *First Break All the Rules: What the World's Greatest Managers Do Differently.* New York: Simon & Schuster, 1999.

Lombardo, Michael M. and Eichinger, Robert W. *Eighty-Eight Assignments for Development in Place.* A study available from the Center for Creative Leadership. See contact information in previous section.

Patterson, Kerry, Grenny, Joseph, McMillan, Ron, Switzler, Al and Covey, Stephen R. *Crucial Conversations: Tools for Talking When Stakes are High.* New York: McGraw-Hill/Contemporay Books, 2002.

Tifft, Susan E. and Jones, Alex S. *The Trust: The Private and Powerful Family Behind* The New York Times. Boston: Little, Brown & Company, 1999.

# *Notes*

1. Gibbon, Ann and Peter Hadekel. *Steinberg: The Breakup of a Family Empire*. Toronto: Macmillan of Canada, 1990.

2. Blondel, C., Carlock, R.S., & Van der Heyden, L. 2001. *Fair Process: Striving for Justice in Family Firms*. Working Paper no. 2001/54/ENT, INSTEAD, Fontainebleau, France.

3. Powell, Horace B. *The Original Has This Signature–W.K. Kellogg*. Englewood Cliffs: Prentice-Hall, p. 198

4. Ibid., p. 202

5. *Developing Family Business Policies: Your Guide to the Future* by Craig E. Aronoff, Ph.D., Joseph H. Astrachan, Ph.D., and John L. Ward, Ph.D. Marietta, GA: Family Enterprise Publishers, ©1998 www.efamilybusiness.com

6. Tifft, Susan E. and Alex S. Jones. *The Trust: The Private and Powerful Family Behind* The New York Times. Boston: Little, Brown and Co., 1999 p. 639

7. "Mentoring in Family Firms: A reflective analysis of senior executives' perceptions" by John Boyd, Nancy Upton and Michelle Wircenski. *Family Business Review*, 12:4, December 1999, pp. 299-310.

8. *Family Business Values: How To Assure a Legacy of Continuity and Success* by Craig E. Aronoff, Ph.D. and John L. Ward, Ph.D. Marietta, GA: Family Enterprise Publishers, ©2001. www.efamilybusiness.com

9. *Making Sibling Teams Work: The Next Generation* by Craig E. Aronoff, Ph.D., Joseph H. Astrachan, Ph.D., Drew S. Mendoza and John L. Ward, Ph.D. Marietta, GA: Family Enterprise Publishers ©1997. www.efamilybusiness.com

10. *Family Business Ownership: How to Be An Effective Shareholder* by Craig E. Aronoff, Ph.D. and John L. Ward, Ph.D. Marietta, GA: Family Enterprise Publishers ©2001. www.efamilybusiness.com

11. *Conflict and Communication in the Family Business* by Joseph H. Astrachan, Ph.D. and Kristi S. McMillan. Marietta, GA: Family Enterprise Publishers ©2003. www.efamilybusiness.com

# Index

# The Author

**Amy M. Schuman,** a senior associate of The Family Business Consulting Group Inc.<sup>sm</sup>, works with family businesses on leadership development, communication skills and team building. Her experience centers on helping family members collaboratively create systems, structures and relationships to help them function as effective stewards of their enterprise. Amy creates leadership and career development approaches tailored for sibling teams, young adults, teens and younger children in the next generation. She helps create conditions for successful generational transfer.

For more than 11 years, Ms. Schuman directed organization development efforts for one of the top 10 of the 100 Best Companies to Work for in America and a fourth-generation, family-owned and managed business. A key executive during the successful transition from third- to fourth-generation family management, she worked closely with the owning families to preserve the company's unique culture, while re-interpreting and updating company practices to meet the intense demands of an increasingly competitive marketplace.

Ms. Schuman has been an adjunct faculty member at Loyola University Chicago's Family Business Center since 1996. She serves as a coach and facilitator in Loyola's Next Generation Leadership Institute, an intensive, two-year program, during which men and women who desire to assume leadership positions in their family businesses are coached in developing leadership skills. She also facilitates a monthly Peer Lab where participants explore the unique challenges of family business leadership. Ms. Schuman teaches group process and facilitation skills in Loyola's Family Business Communication Institute and leads Chicago's only support group for women in family business.

Ms. Schuman has made presentations at the Family Firm Institute Conference and the Family Business Network meeting in Stockholm, Sweden. She has been an adjunct faculty member of the Lake Forest College Graduate School of Management and has taught at the University of Illinois, Chicago Campus, MBA program. She has a B.A. in Psychology from Oberlin College and has completed work towards a Master's Degree in Organization Development.

Ms. Schuman currently lives in the Chicago area with her husband, a clinical psychologist, and their three children.